One day Mr. B was holding his book upside down and I realized he couldn't see well enough to read any longer. Ever so gently, I offered to read to him. Instantly offended, he sputtered angrily, "Can't you see I *am* reading?"

I felt a deep sadness. *Not by might nor by power, but by My Spirit*, I seemed to hear the Lord remind me. Again I prayed silently, as I so often did.

"You know the rules!" Miss Rosie thundered, and I nodded miserably.

"There will be no lipstick! No rouge at the Norwegian American Hospital. And to think you have lipstick and rouge on, Miss Tweten. You should be ashamed!"

"No. Oh, no," I protested. "I never wear rouge or lipstick.

"Now, you are lying!"

"Oh, no! I'm not lying. I don't even have any lipstick or rouge."

"We'll see!" Miss Rosie towered over me now as she grabbed a washcloth and proceeded to scrub my face. I felt my cheeks burning but the cloth was clean.

Other books by Margaret Jensen

First We Have Coffee

Lena

First Comes the Wind

Papa's Place

Violets
for Mister B

Margaret Jensen

Here's Life Publishers

First printing, July 1988
Second printing, November 1988

Published by
HERE'S LIFE PUBLISHERS, INC.
P. O. Box 1576
San Bernardino, CA 92402

Library of Congress Cataloging-in-Publication Data

Jensen, Margaret T. (Margaret Tweten), 1916-
  Violets for Mr. B.

  1. Jensen, Margaret T. (Margaret Tweten),
1916-   . 2. Christian biography—United States.
I. Title.
BR1725.J43A3   1988   209'.2'4 [B]   88-664
ISBN 0-89840-211-5 (pbk.)

Scripture quotations are from the *King James Version.*

Chapter 1 has been adapted from an article which appeared in
Moody Monthly (April 1985). Used by permission.

For More Information, Write:

L.I.F.E. —P.O. Box A399, Sydney South 2000, Australia
Campus Crusade for Christ of Canada —Box 300, Vancouver, B.C., V6C 2X3, Canada
Campus Crusade for Christ —Pearl Assurance House, 4 Temple Row, Birmingham, B2 5HG,
England
Lay Institute for Evangelism —P.O. Box 8786, Auckland 3, New Zealand
Campus Crusade for Christ —P.O. Box 240, Colombo Court Post Office, Singapore 9117
Great Commission Movement of Nigeria —P.O. Box 500, Jos, Plateau State Nigeria, West Africa
Campus Crusade for Christ International —Arrowhead Springs, San Bernardino CA, 92414, U.S.A.

DEDICATED TO:

MY CLASSMATES:
Hertha Nielsen Petersen, R.N.
Betty Schweitzer Wilson, R.N.
Gladys Thompson Ellefsen, R.N.

MY GRANDCHILDREN:
Heather Carlberg
Chad Carlberg
Shawn Jensen
Eric Jensen
Sarah Jensen
Kathryn Jensen

My prayer is that my grandchildren will
glean from the past
grow in the present
give to the future

SPECIAL THANKS

To Leslie H. Stobbe, Wayne Hastings, Dan Benson, Jean Bryant, and all the staff at Here's Life Publishers, Inc., for believing that "all things are possible."

To my Harold, my husband of 50 years, who types in the dining room while I write in the kitchen. In addition, he is hammering nails to build a hideaway. He, too, believes in miracles.

To my children: Janice and Judson Carlberg and Ralph and Chris Jensen, who continue to amaze me as they work and grow together to establish strong family ties that bind the past generations and the present together. They bring hope for the future.

To all those doctors and nurses whom I had the privilege to work with. I learned from each one. Since there are too many to name, I will mention just three doctors from each place.

From Chicago (50 years ago): Dr. Thornton, Dr. Schroeder and Dr. C. David Brown.

From Marietta, Georgia: Dr. R. Clark, Dr. Benson and Dr. Fred Schmidt.

From Greensboro, North Carolina: Dr. James Bruce, Dr. Frank Brown and Dr. Russel Lyday.

From Wilmington, North Carolina: Dr. B. Williams, Dr. Robert Hutchins and Dr. Luke Sampson.

Thank you.
Margaret Jensen

CONTENTS

INTRODUCTION

At the earliest sign of spring, Mama took us to the woods near the Quaker Oats Company in Saskatoon, Saskatchewan, to gather the first violets of April. To Mama the flower symbolized hope and warm breezes and sun-filled days.

Even when some late snowflakes fell, the blue and purple faces of the violets managed to peek through the snow — a reminder that the long winter was past and the flowers of summer were on the way. Giddy with expectation, we carried our violets home in a basket, then placed them in a bowl and waited for the promise of summer.

Many years later violets again reminded me of the promise of life after a cold winter of death. Professional and vibrant in my starched white nurse's uniform, I reached out to a dying patient. I placed a bowl of violets on the windowsill in Mr. B's room — violets that still remain on the dusty ledges of my memory — a reminder that the spring of hope defies the winter of the soul.

VIOLETS FOR MR. B will bring a bowl of spring violets to your windowsill. With it comes hope for your tomorrow.

1

VIOLETS FOR MR. B

He swept the view with his thin blue hand. "All of this used to be woods," he said. "We used to pick violets in the spring. Now the woods are way out there, beyond the parking lots!"

The doctor's phone call was on my mind as I threw a white sweater over my new uniform. "A prominent man has returned from New York to his home town to die," the doctor said. "He desires no visitors, flowers or conversation. He is a bitter, lonely man—and gravely ill. Do what you can, Margaret."

I gathered my nurse's bag, bulging with credentials, equipment, New Testament, *Reader's Digest,* pen and paper.

Traffic was light at 6:15 A.M. I gave myself enough time to park, register at the hospital office, and get a

13

report from the night nurse.

Inside the gloomy room, a gaunt, hollow-eyed man was propped up in bed with a book in front of him. With a curt, "Good morning," Mr. B resumed his reading.

I sat in a corner and quietly read the chart, trying to get my bearings as to how to care for this independent, brusque man. *Help, Lord!* I prayed silently.

He seemed to enjoy my discomfort. Once he offered a suggestion: "Don't try so hard, Mrs. Jensen."

Within a few days we had set up a comfortable routine. At first I tried conversation that stemmed from the *Reader's Digest* or current books—a good beginning, I thought. He knew most of the writers. Then I decided to brighten his day with some stories from the *National Geographic*. He said he had already been to those places. I bit my lip.

He seemed to enjoy my discomfort. Once he offered a suggestion: "Don't try so hard, Mrs. Jensen."

I burst out laughing and agreed just to be his friend and do things his way. The tension lessened.

When ministers or boyhood acquaintances came to call, he insisted I observe the "No Visitors" sign. The only visitor he received was his sister, who came every day to relieve me for lunch. She and her brother rarely spoke. She would sit quietly beside him and just read.

One day she said, "I can do so little for my brother,

Mrs. Jensen. He was so assertive and successful and I'm just a quiet wife and mother. I wish I could be more like him, yet I'm really content to be what I am."

"Oh, if you only knew how much gentle people can bless others," I said to her. "They're refreshing, like quiet streams and green meadows. Your actions speak louder than words when you come day after day to sit with your brother. You communicate your love, and he hears."

She stared out the window, her lower lip trembling.

My conversation with Mr. B became more relaxed as I related humorous incidents from my family. One day I told Mr. B about my son, Ralph, and how during his childhood he once came running in from play and said, "Mommy, Mommy, how do I explain to God why I was bad when I should have been good?"

"Oh, you don't have to explain to God," I told Ralph. "He knows all about us. Remember that song in Sunday school that said, 'Jesus paid it all, all to Him I owe'? When we confess our sins, Ralph, He forgives us."

"Oh, good!" my son said. "I forgot that part." Then he ran out to play.

It soon became routine to see Mr. B look over his glasses and say, "Well?" That meant he was ready for another story, usually a humorous one about Ralph. I was on familiar ground there, and I realized my stories opened a new world to my cynical patient.

One morning he did the routine, "Well?" But he added, "What does the theologian, Ralph, say today?"

15

"Come to think of it," I said, "he did make a theological observation yesterday. When we passed an old Model-T Ford, he said, 'Well, Mom, it's not the car that counts, it's the driver in it. That car won't go far without a driver. Kinda like us, huh? Our bodies wear out, but we live on, right? It's the soul that counts.'"

At a later date, I even ventured to take my record player and some classical records into Mr. B's room. He listened patiently for a few days, but finally, in exasperation, he exploded. "I enjoy music only in concert halls — not canned!"

I dragged my *canned music* to the parking lot.

One day he was holding his book upside down and I realized he couldn't see well enough to read any longer. Ever so gently, I offered to read to him. Instantly offended, he sputtered angrily, "Can't you see I *am* reading?"

I felt a deep sadness. *Not by might nor by power, but by My Spirit*, I seemed to hear the Lord remind me. Again I prayed silently, as I so often did.

When a card came from New York, I read the verse and note from his former secretary. She said she had paid to have prayers said for him.

Mr. B struggled to maintain his composure. "She thought enough of me to pay for prayers?"

"God thought enough of you to send His Son to die for you," I said softly, then slipped out of the room before he could argue. When I returned, he was holding the card.

Looking out the window, he swept the view with

16

his thin blue hand. "All of this used to be woods," he said. "We used to pick violets in the spring. Now the woods are way out there, beyond the parking lots and I can't even see the violets. I'm glad I can still see the birds and squirrels, though."

His tone had lost its bitterness. Only sadness remained. I told him about gathering violets with Mama in the springtime. He nodded solemnly.

After a while, each day found him weaker, and he had to be turned in bed. He no longer held his book.

One day a gentle knock on the door interrupted my thoughts. When I opened the door, a beautiful woman stood there, holding a bowl of violets. "Would you tell Mr. B that I'm one of those children who used to play in the woods when he did, and pick violets? I know he doesn't want visitors or flowers, but I thought he might like these."

I thanked her and took the flowers from her. I placed them on the window sill and turned Mr. B to face the sky and woods. When I told him about the visitor at the door, he stared at the violets.

"The violets were dead last winter," I said, "but now it's spring and these are alive. Jesus said, 'I am the resurrection and the life; he who believes in Me shall live even if he dies.' Do you believe this?"

I went about my duties. I knew he heard me, but I didn't wait for an answer.

A day came when I sat beside Mr. B and held his cold, frail hands. Softly I said the Lord's Prayer and his lips followed my words. Again I said to him, "Jesus said, 'I am the resurrection and the life; he who believes in

Me shall live.'" I looked into his face. "Do you believe this, Mr. B?"

"Turn me to the window," he whispered. After turning him, I put a pillow behind his back to prop him up.

Looking at the violets, he whispered, "I believe."

I sat back down beside him. Tears blinded my eyes.

"It's all right now," he said. "I believe."

Quietly, gently, Mr. B slipped into his final sleep— and out of the wintry darkness and despair of his heart into joy and everlasting life.

2

A TIME TO REMEMBER

---

*My drawer was empty, and a brown box
on the bed held all my belongings.
Nothing would ever be the same.*

Nostalgia almost choked me that February morning in 1934 as I looked around the small bedroom where I had shared a bed with my sisters, Grace and Doris. My eyes settled momentarily on the lone dresser with its three drawers. There was barely enough space in the room to open the drawers, and now I had emptied one of them. Grace and Doris could divide the extra drawer.

The room was filled with Mama's loving touches—flowered curtains, and a matching coverlet on a woolen quilt that Mama had pieced together from the Jewish merchant's sample scraps of cloth. When the merchant brought the samples Mama had a cup of coffee waiting. They talked about the "old country," their children, and their hopes for the future in the "new world."

Gingerly, I pushed back the bedroom curtains and stared out on Mama's new world — the brick wall of the neighbor's flat and beyond that, somewhere, the streets and alleys of Chicago. As I fingered the curtains, I remembered how Mama went to the Logan Department Store and bought the flowered material for ten cents a yard. When I returned from school one day, there were the new curtains and the old quilt was covered in matching material. The small room was alive with color, and it didn't seem to matter that the brick wall of the next flat was our only view from the window.

So many memories flooded in with the early evening breeze. On Fridays, the fish man peddled his wares, shouting, "Fresh fish . . . fresh fish . . . " As his horse-drawn cart neared the house, Mama would run down two flights of stairs to get to the cart before it was gone. How often Mama and the neighbor Mrs. Andreason sipped coffee and laughed about the day the fish peddler beat his tired horse heartlessly as he moved down the alley.

An elderly lady in a second floor flat leaned over the porch railing, bellowing, "Have you no mercy?"

In response, the old man yelled back, "No — only fish, fresh fish."

Standing at my bedroom window, I remembered how Chicago alleys played their music to housewives who leaned over porches or stood at pulley lines hanging clothes that waved and flapped to peddlers below. Not far behind the fish peddler came the shrill ringing of a bell. "Ragsaline . . . ragsaline . . . ," echoed against the Chicago flats. "Rags and any old iron" kept in tune with "Fresh fish, fresh fish."

The sounds, and the sights, and the smells all blended together, and the symphony was kept alive by the chattering and yelling of the housewives as they gathered rags and scraps of old iron for the peddler. In return, he dropped pennies into their hands—pennies that would buy fresh fish. Haggling over prices was a form of entertainment not to be taken lightly.

Shy Mama announced to the desk clerk—
and to everyone within hearing distance—
"This is my daughter, Margaret Tweten,
and she is going to be a nurse."

Mingled with the other sounds was the comforting clip-clop from a tired old horse as children scurried to collect sugar lumps from Scandinavian sugar bowls. Without traffic lights, the shaggy horses pulled on their carts past the peddlers who were on foot, carrying their wares, and around the children as they played kick the can in the street.

When school was out, the summer sounds of the organ grinder and his monkey blended with the bells from the Good Humor man. But Mama's children knew better than to follow those bells. Two Good Humor bars meant ten cents worth of bologna, and that was enough for supper in the Tweten home.

Finally, I turned back and faced my bedroom. I looked at the starched embroidered scarf that covered the stains on the worn dresser. Our Sunday school

Bibles were on the cloth. Now my drawer was empty, and a brown box on the bed held all my belongings. Nothing would ever be the same.

My fingers trembled as I put my hat on, tilting it slightly to the right like Leona did. I studied myself in the mirror and glowed with pride at my new silk dress and my new brown coat with its fur collar. Leona Ghertsen, a nurse friend, had taken me to Marshal Fields in Oak Park to buy my high school graduation gift: my first store-bought dress, my first pair of high-heeled pumps, and new silk stockings. I knew I would love Leona forever.

The soft brown coat was a gift from Mrs. Knight, a lovely white-haired lady from Papa's church. Slowly, I collected my scarf and gloves and the purse that matched. Then I picked up my brown box and closed the bedroom door behind me without looking back.

Downstairs, Grace and Doris had finished the supper dishes and Mama gave some last minute instructions about the younger children, Joyce and Jeanelle. Gordon was practicing the violin, its not-too-melodious sound filling the room. Papa looked up and said, "Ja, ja, Margaret—so you are growing up!" Without another word, he returned to his study and books.

Silently, methodically, Mama buttoned her long black coat, pulled her hat on firmly, wrapped a woolen scarf around her neck and slipped her woolen gloves over her thin fingers. Smiling, my nurse friend Leona buttoned up her fur coat, tilted her hat to the right, tucked a silk scarf around the collar, and carefully pulled on long kid gloves.

By then my sisters and brother were standing around me in quiet awe. With quick hugs and a lump building in my throat, I carried the box down the steps and Mama, Leona and I walked in silence to the Fullerton Avenue street car.

Leona and Mama talked about many things and I held my box tightly on my lap until the Division Avenue streetcar stopped. We walked against the Chicago wind to 1044 Francisco Avenue and paused. The sign read: Norwegian American Hospital. We marched up the stone steps and through the massive doors — Mama and Leona walking proudly.

Then Mama, shy Mama, announced to the desk clerk — and to everyone within hearing distance — "This young lady is my daughter, Margaret Tweten, and she is going to be a nurse."

3

ROOM 200

The room was too quiet. The lump in my throat got bigger.

Mama and Leona walked back down the hall, turned and waved, and then slipped quietly out of sight. I was alone—alone in room 200. The large windows overlooked the street below where red brick flats huddled together to brace against the Chicago wind. Across the hall was the fire escape.

My lonely box sat on one of the twin metal beds. I realized I would sleep alone for the first time in my life. Yet I was not entirely alone, for my roommate, Hertha Nielsen, a high school friend, was due to arrive at any moment. Two metal desks and two chairs, along with a large wastepaper basket, were lined up against a white wall. In the corner was a sink with white towels hanging on a rack.

The dressers intrigued me when I realized that

each of us had a separate one, and each one had three large drawers. A dresser of my own! How would I ever fill it?

The room was too quiet. The lump in my throat got bigger. Then I remembered a day when I was twelve and came home from school and told Mama how mixed up the world was getting. I told her how I had a crush on Art. And I told her that Art liked my friend, Eleanor, but Eleanor liked somebody else, who in turn liked somebody else. I said, "Oh, Mama, I could die!"

"Ja, ja," she answered patiently. "While you are dying—iron!"

She proceeded to pull a basket of ironing from under the kitchen table and while I ironed I forgot about dying. I was too tired. Besides, Mama had meatballs and a chocolate cake for supper.

Now, alone in that big dorm room, I felt again like I could die. I was so lonesome. So I had to "iron"—I had to do something! So I turned to the box on the bed and began to empty it even though all my possessions would fill only one dresser drawer.

Papa had tied a good knot so it took me a while to get the box open. Once it was open, I took out the black cotton stockings from the Logan Department Store and the black oxfords that were still in their shoebox. All of that could go in one drawer. Later I would get the uniforms I had already been measured for.

The lump in my throat began to go away. I took out the new pajamas, one of the gifts from the young people at Papa's church. There was new underwear, three new cotton slips, and cotton stockings, along with

25

the pair of silk hose which I was wearing.

I hung my two skirts and blouses and my beautiful new store-bought coat with the fur collar in the closet beside my new bathrobe. Later I would hang the silk dress I was wearing in the closet beside my coat.

It was like reliving the church party all over again when I took the gifts of love, one by one, and placed them in the large drawers.

The beautiful wrist watch I was wearing, a real nurse's watch with a second hand, was a gift from the young people of the Logan Square Norwegian Baptist Church of Chicago. It had been wrapped in layers of paper, placed in a large box and then ceremoniously presented to me by the president, Nils Olsen. My expression of joy brought forth a burst of laughter as we were caught up together in that golden moment of friendship.

From the box I took the pen and pencil set and placed them on the metal desk beside a box of floral stationery. I hid the diary under my underwear. The bedside table was a perfect place for my Bible and my devotional book, *Streams in the Desert*. I opened the pages of the devotional and read the inscription:

Happy Birthday, Margaret

From Eleanor Holby — April 18, 1932.

I wrote:

February 19, 1934
Entered Norwegian American Hospital
Training School.

In the top drawer I placed the fancy handkerchiefs

and the lavender soap and powder. My comb and brush, scrubbed clean, were placed beside my box of curved combs that I used at night to make waves in my blond hair. I had to tie a ribbon around the combs every night to hold those elusive waves in place. How I envied Eleanor's wavy hair! I would pull my hair back in a low knot so the waves would cover my ears. No foolish "kiss curls" on my forehead! Papa saw to that!

Best of all, Mrs. Nielsen unwrapped her Danish cakes and cookies. We were going to have a party!

In my hand I held a wall plaque, a gift from my gentle friend, Mary, with the words by Annie Johnson Flint:

He giveth more grace
When the burdens grow greater.

Unable to go to school, gentle Mary played with her dolls as the years rolled by. Mama suggested that I play "house" with my lonely friend, so for a few hours I would become a young child and play dolls with Mary. When I said good-bye she held the gift of love in her hand while her mother cried. I wondered who would play with my special friend.

Tucked into my flannel nightgown was a mystery package. When I opened it, there was a box of fudge from Grace, Gordon, Doris, Joy Solveig, and Jeanelle. Before my eyes I saw them delightedly scraping the bowl clean, but not daring to touch any of "Margaret's surprise present." The lump suddenly came back into my throat, and sobs exploded in the lonely room.

I washed my face and hid the fudge in my drawer just before Hertha arrived on the scene. Her father and brother carried her suitcases in.

I marveled as I watched my roommate fill the closet with beautiful clothes and moan over the lack of space. Sharing a room would be an adventure for Hertha.

Her adoring mother brought some beautiful accessories to decorate the barren room.

Best of all, the jovial, plump Mrs. Nielsen unwrapped her Danish cakes and cookies. We were going to have a party! Hertha, good-natured like her mother, laughingly took command over the stark bleakness of white walls and metal beds. She cleared her desk for our party just before Betty Schweitzer, another high school friend who had entered training in September, came in. Betty was getting off her twelve-hour shift — 7:30 to 7:30. I would soon discover that by the time the charts were finished, it could be 8:30!

The sounds of showers, laughing nurses who were off duty now and footsteps running up and down the hall were friendly greetings for the new students in room 200.

A senior nurse came to welcome us. Other new students had already gathered in our room for Hertha's party but the Senior nurse reminded us that, "Lights go out at 10 P.M.—sharp." She also instructed us to be in chapel at 6:45 A.M., and at breakfast by 7, then to report to Miss Rosendahl's office at 7:30. We shuddered!

Hertha's touch had transformed the barren room into a place of warm coziness. The cookies and cakes that were left were packed safely in tins for another day. Hertha's family said goodnight; the day was coming to a quiet close. We set the alarm clock for 6 A.M. and at 10 P.M. our lights were out.

In the darkness — alone in my single metal bed — I wondered if Grace and Doris missed me like I missed them.

Hertha turned the radio low and Wayne King's "The Waltz You Saved For Me" floated with me into my dreams.

We never heard Miss Abrahamson's footsteps as she came down the hall for bed check. We were much too weary.

4

MISS ROSIE

I suspected her goal in life was to send forth the Florence Nightingales of tomorrow, but we saw "Rosie" as the general — and we were the war zone!

An early morning sun tried vainly to filter through the cold, predawn darkness of Chicago. The radiators crackled and popped with a vengeance, sending steam upward from the drying underwear, spread over the towel-covered radiators.

Hertha and I dressed quickly in the cold dawn, pulling on new underwear, long cotton slips, black cotton stockings and shiny oxfords. With a sense of awe, we slipped into our blue-and-white striped uniforms. Over those long uniforms we awkwardly fastened our starched white pinafores and buttoned on stiff collars and cuffs. We were excited, nervous, giggling.

30

I brushed back my hair in a soft bun and the waves stayed in place. Hertha's curly dark hair framed her round cheeks and mischievous brown eyes. She shifted her ample frame into the snug pinafore.

I inspected my carefully trimmed and cleaned fingernails, wound my shiny new wrist watch and clipped a fountain pen in place in my pocket beside the bandage scissors and clean handkerchief.

We checked our room to see that all was in order: Bed made, sink cleaned, wastebasket emptied. During the week, we would get a dust mop from down the hall to dust the floors and on Saturday we would scrub our room. But not today.

The sound of laughter and footsteps erupted in the hall. We stepped from room 200 and followed the older nurses to the chapel. The ones with three black bands on their starched caps were seniors and they went first. The two-black-stripers were second-year students and the one-stripe cap meant a one-year student. Plain caps were given after the three-month probationary period. We came up last — all the new students — with bare heads. Our starched uniforms rustled in tune with the others and we quietly filled the chapel.

Miss Rosendahl, director of nurses, seemed majestic — tall, broad, overpowering. Her flaming red hair was piled high on her head, a starched cap on top of that. She wore a long, stiff uniform and a wide belt around her ample hips. But it was the way she stood — like a general, with folded arms, feet apart and her clear blue eyes taking in every minute detail. I knew right then and there that no one missed chapel.

In her commanding voice, Miss Rosendahl an-

nounced a hymn. Miss Johnson, a petite blonde called
Johnnie, sat at the piano. Miss Rosendahl's voice rang
out with one of her favorite hymns:

> Holy Ghost with light divine,
> Shine upon this heart of mine.

When she came to the part, "Bid my many woes
depart," I somehow sensed she meant us. She never
quite made the high notes, but she made up for it with
her fervor. Chapel ended with a Scripture verse and the
Lord's Prayer, and we moved out, according to rank.
This time "Miss Rosie" marched in the lead and I had
a feeling that we should be singing:

> Onward Christian soldiers
> Marching as to war.

The rustling probationers—the new "probies"—
without caps—brought up the rear.

Breakfast was eaten hurriedly since the nurses
reported on their floors at 7:30 A.M.—but our "capless"
band headed for Miss Rosendahl's office where we met
the director of nurses personally. A former war nurse,
she looked at us as though we were still at war. I
suspected that underneath that stern exterior was a
dedicated nurse whose goal in life was to send forth the
Florence Nightingales of tomorrow. That day, though,
we young students saw "Rosie" as the general, and ourselves as the war zone.

With arms folded, she met our fears with a firm
gaze. "Discipline, my children [I was seventeen!]; yes,
my children [emphasis on children], discipline! You
must learn to take orders and follow them." Her eyes
met mine. I wanted to say, "Haven't I lived with Papa?"

I sucked in my lower lip as she continued, "Lives

are at stake in this hospital and you hold those lives in your hands. By one error you can send a person into eternity. Yes, girls, discipline is what I will have!"

I shuddered! A life in my hand was awesome.

"I will stand for no nonsense," she said firmly. "And the breaking of rules will send you packing—yes, I mean packing! Home in disgrace!"

I visualized my box being repacked and me heading home to face Papa. Oh, I would obey the rules—no mistaking that!

"Miss Tweten, come into my office at once!" Rosie ordered. I looked at Hertha— terrified! What had I done?

Our first assignment was to clean the closets on different floors. Hertha and I rearranged linens and scrubbed shelves as though our lives depended upon those linen closets. Then we were taught how to make beds, and we practiced for hours until the corners could pass Miss Rosie's inspection.

During one boring session of making and remaking beds, Hertha picked up a book and read to me about "Anthony whispering sweet nothings into Cleopatra's shell-pink ear." With all the drama of a Hollywood star, Hertha was acting out the dramatic scene—and Miss Rosie came in to check the corners.

I never did find out what "sweet nothings" went into Cleopatra's shell-pink ear, but I still remember the lecture on discipline versus nonsense.

In between the practical work assignments, we attended four hours of classes a day. With our new books and notebooks tucked under our arms, we marched to class to hear lectures from doctors and to learn "practical nursing" from graduate nurses.

Dr. G taught Materia Medica and he promised to fail any student who did not know the measurements "frontward and backward." We dreaded his exams, particularly those on measurements, but no one ever failed them. His students were known to score high on state board exams.

The days moved quickly through three months, and then came the capping ceremony when Miss Rosie planted our plain starched caps firmly on our heads. At last we were called student nurses, not just probies. We had arrived! I had missed picking the springtime violets with Mama and the children but I had a cap on my head.

Unexpectedly, one day I was in trouble with the director of nurses. "Miss Tweten, come into my office at once!" She ordered. I looked at Hertha—I was terrified. What had I done? Hertha's sympathetic gaze followed me, but then the door closed and I was alone with Miss Rosie.

"You know the rules, Miss Tweten." Her voice rose. "I have a good mind to call your father—and you a minister's daughter."

I shuddered! *Papa? What did he have to do with this?*

"You know the rules," she thundered again and I nodded miserably.

"There will be no lipstick! No rouge at the Norwegian American Hospital. And to think you have lipstick and rouge on, Miss Tweten. You should be ashamed!"

"No. Oh, no," I protested. "I never wear rouge or lipstick. Papa won't let us."

"Now, you are lying! I will call your father."

"Oh, no! I'm not lying. I don't even have any lipstick or rouge." My cheeks felt hot.

"We'll see!" Miss Rosie towered over me now as she grabbed a washcloth and proceeded to scrub my face. I felt my cheeks burning but the cloth was clean. A frown split her brow. Her expression seemed puzzled as she looked at my red cheeks and red lips and mut-tered, "I can't believe it—it looked like lipstick." She squared her shoulders even more. "Well, well, well," she added in conciliatory tones. "What kind of soap do you use?"

"Anything Mama finds on sale," I stammered.

"Now you are impudent!" Her eyes blazed.

"Oh, no, Miss Rosendahl, I really mean it. Mama likes Palmolive, but she will get other soap on sale." I was trembling inside. I didn't want to pack up and go home. Awkwardly I said, "Dr. Thornton says I have a good complexion because I walk all the time. I walked to Carl Schurz High School from Logan Square and on my afternoon off from the hospital I walk home."

"My gracious, child, that is four to five miles."

I winced. She had called me "child." Didn't she know that I was seventeen? Meekly I said, "I enjoy walking, Miss Rosendahl. Besides I don't have 5 cents

35

for carfare. Papa brings me back, so that saves 10 cents."

She looked away. "Well, time's wasting. Get back to work, Miss Tweten, and no nonsense."

"Oh, no, Miss Rosendahl, no nonsense." I almost danced back to my room, though that was against the rules, too. But all I could think of was, *I don't have to pack! I don't have to pack! Oh, glory! Life is good!*

Later, behind closed doors, I gave a one-woman show, and Betty and Hertha rocked with laughter. Word soon spread throughout the dormitory that Rosie had washed my face.

Later in the week when I had my half-day off, I walked through Humbolt Park and once again found myself in Mama's warm kitchen. The children gathered around me and Papa was quietly impressed as I told about the classes and floor training — and Miss Rosendahl.

Mama's hot meatballs and gravy, her mashed potatoes, and creamed peas and carrots never tasted so good.

5

FOURTH FLOOR ANNEX

The doctor turned to me and ordered,
"Give her the 'three H's'"—That meant a
soapsuds enema—high, hot, and a "h" of
a lot.

By the time I was assigned to Fourth Floor Annex, I had the stripe on my cap, and routine days of floor duty and study had blended into months of discipline and learning. With the discipline came a degree of responsibility, a growing confidence, and a sense of pride in my work. I loved what I was doing. I was an idealistic, romantic eighteen-year-old "child" according to Miss Rosie, but I loved people and I learned from them even though they demanded much from me.

Miss Hanna, the head nurse of Fourth Annex, was my first introduction to Fourth Medical. She was a slender, dark-haired woman in starched white from cap to shoelaces—a picture of efficiency. Her dark eyes were hauntingly beautiful and I wondered if they concealed a hidden romantic behind the starched exterior. Miss Hanna seemed to soften the assignment to Fourth Medical where we faced life at its best and its worst; we saw its humor and pathos, its courage and cowardice. Most of all, it was a test of endurance — long hours and hard, physical work, tending patients who were bedridden and seriously ill. For many the hospital stay was their last resort because they were terminal. The doctors, nurses and patients, from various ethnic and religious backgrounds, learned to blend together under the extreme pressures. Besides, Miss Hanna was there. She was trusted and respected, and she ran a tight ship. Miss Rosie's years of "discipline" rang through all the hospital corridors and was clearly evident in the lives of her head nurses.

Each morning, at 7:30, Miss Hanna greeted us at the nurses' station. Our day shift, starched and alert, and the night shift, limp and weary-eyed, all stood together to hear the night report. After the report, Miss Hanna posted our assignments and medicine list on the bulletin board.

We student nurses hurriedly collected breakfast trays, lined up for clean linen and began our trek to the utility room for basins, bedpans and enema cans.

One morning I had four patients to tend before my ten o'clock class. While my other patients finished breakfast, I bathed Miss Kari who was slowly dying. Her distended abdomen looked like a full-term pregnancy; blue-grey pallor colored her clammy skin.

Gently, I swabbed her parched mouth with some glycerine and lemon, and coaxed her to swallow a few drops of water. Her haunted dark eyes followed me. While I bathed her, I softly sang some old hymns and assured her of God's love. Then I turned her on her side, placed a pillow behind her back and brushed her long damp hair. I found a ribbon on a plant in the hall and tied her hair with a bow. I took her hands — one at a time — and trimmed and cleaned her fingernails. Then I put her rosary in her hand. She smiled and clutched it to her breast. She moaned in pain, and I administered morphine sulphate.

How do you chart a dying woman, a frightened teenager with a severe tooth infection, or old Grandpa Joe still hollering for the toilet?

I went to the door and nodded to the off-duty policeman waiting in the hall. "You can come in now," I whispered. He eased his 6-foot-6 frame into a chair beside Miss Kari and spoke softly to her in Polish as he took her hand and held it tenderly in his big hand.

He looked up, almost apologetically. "My sister," he said softly. "We came from Poland together." I knew he would still be sitting there at the close of the day. Miss Kari dozed, comfortable and secure in the love of her only relative. I closed the door.

After gathering up the remaining trays, I bathed a nineteen-year-old boy with a severe tooth infection, gave him aspirin to reduce his fever, and applied saline packs around his red, swollen jaw. "You must drink," I urged him, placing a pitcher of juice on his bed stand.

He nodded, his eyes glassy.

By the time I reached Mr. Joe, he was trying to pull out his catheter and yelling for the toilet. "I'll wet this d--- bed if you can't get me to the toilet," he scolded. Finally he was bathed and quieted. Still he glared angrily at the contraption that spilled urine into a bottle. "Fool thing if I ever heard of one," he muttered.

I agreed.

"Blondie! Help me! Help, Blondie!" screamed Mrs. Goldstein down the hall. "Tweedlededum, where are you? Oh, Blondie, help! Help!"

I hurried to Mrs. Goldstein's room with a basin and bedpan in my hands. Her abdomen was distended, too.

"Oye, oye — a doctor you should be getting, Blondie. Call Dr. Finklefish . . . oye, Dr. Finklefish!" she yelled. "Help!"

"Shhh . . . it's not Dr. Finklefish. It's Dr. Finklestein. Dr. Fishskin is the lab extern."

"So? What does that matter, Tweedlededum?"

"Shh. Miss Rosendahl should hear you. Tweedlededum — such a nickname for Miss Tweten."

She ignored my reprimand. "Get Dr. Fishfinkle — or whatever," she persisted. "Can't you see I'm dying?"

The intern, Dr. Finklestein, was down the hall. I hurried to him with Mrs. Goldstein's request. "Please, I have to get to class!" I told him.

When we reached her room, he said, "All right, Mrs. Goldstein, what have you been eating?"

"Choking, I am! Can't you see the cast is choking me? From my legs to my breast — this cast is choking me. A hip I should break — oye, oye! No one should suffer like this. My mother died with a broken hip. But I won't!"

Her distended abdomen had made her hip cast tight as a drum.

"Come on, now, Mrs. Goldstein, be honest. Tell me what you've been eating."

"Isn't it enough that I am dying with a broken hip? I should go to my grave with the malnutrition, too?"

I peered into her bedside table. The doctor's gaze followed mine, settling on the rye bread, chicken bones, jars of pickled herring, and cheese and pickles.

Dr. Finklestein moaned, "Oh, no! And how many times have I told you not to eat anything besides your diet? These foods make so much gas, and you'll gain too much weight."

"So . . . a little bite now and then to keep up my strength?" She moaned miserably to emphasize her plight.

Turning to me, he ordered, "Give her the three H's." That meant a soapsuds enema — high, hot, and a "h" of a lot.

I wouldn't dare use the word Papa used in his sermons.

I ran to the utility room, leaving Mrs. G muttering about it being bad enough to have a broken hip but now she'd go to her grave with the malnutrition.

I recruited some help, and we turned the mountainous body (cast and patient) amid screams of, "I'm dying! Help! Help!" I held up the white enamel can filled with soapsuds made from left over scraps of soap, and inserted the long red rubber tubing—high, hot and a "h" of a lot.

We planted the still screaming Mrs. Goldstein on the bedpan and used newspaper to protect the linens. I prayed, "Please, Lord, not the entire bed. I have class in 20 minutes."

While she sat on the bedpan, I ran to check the other patients, then back to Mrs. Goldstein in response to her cry, "Blondie! Blondie!"

Sure enough, the distention was down, and Mrs. Goldstein decided to live. One of the nurses came in to help, and between the two of us, we got Mrs. G bathed, powdered and into a clean bed, with a silly ribbon in her hair for good measure.

"So . . . a nap I'll take," she said, patting her cast. "You'll be a good nurse someday, Tweedlededum."

Back at the nurses station, I scrubbed vigorously, then gathered up my books for class. It was ten o'clock. I had made it!

After lunch I had two more classes, then back to the Fourth Floor Annex for scheduled P.M. care. Basins came out again. Faces and hands were washed. Beds were straightened. Back rubs given and supper trays cleared. Then, bedpans before the visitors came.

As the night crew came on at 7:30, I took my charts to a corner and sat down. But how do you chart a dying woman, a frightened teenager with a severe tooth infection or old Grandpa Joe still hollering for the toilet?

How do you ever chart Mrs. Goldstein? They just stay etched in your memories.

Thirty minutes later I put down my charts and wearily headed for my room on the second floor of the dorm. The nurses lived on one side and the interns lived on the other side. A wide hall — and honor — stood between us.

I showered, put on clean pajamas and a robe. Someone in the kitchen made a pot of tea and Hertha and I had a party. Then we studied for Dr. B's exam on Materia Medica to the sound of waltz music. Mama might not have approved of all the waltzes, but then it was Hertha's radio and Hertha didn't have to listen to Moody Bible's radio station.

6

NIGHT WATCH

I reassured Mrs. Olsen that the long night would pass and by morning she would be better. I was trying to reassure both of us.

After getting our 7:30 report and checking the medicine lists, our P.M. cares began by emptying waste baskets and passing out fresh water until the visitors left. Then came back rubs, and we changed draw sheets, washed each patient's face and hands, and helped each one with oral hygiene. The cart with bedpans rattled down the hall toward the utility room where the pans would be emptied and washed. I ran the halls trying to keep up with the demands of forty patients, most of them on complete bed rest.

Medicines, including sleeping pills, were carefully checked and administered. Most of our patients had been cared for in their homes until they became too ill, and now the hospital was a place of fear for them. So part of our care was to tuck the more frightened ones in for the night. Lights were turned low and the flowers and plants were taken out of the rooms and placed in the hall to be watered and returned before the morning shift.

One particular night, Miss Hanna urged me to hurry. A new patient was in the corner isolation room: diagnosis — erysipelas. I knew what that meant — an acute infectious disease of the skin or mucous membranes caused by a streptococcus and characterized by inflammation and fever.

Grabbing a broom I began to "chase rats" at my patient's direction.

I put on my isolation gown, mask and gloves and entered the room to care for my patient. She was in pain as I applied fresh dressings to the oozing lesions that covered her face and body. It was lonely in her room. The patient — her face wrapped in gauze, her eyes full of pain — haunted me. So I stopped long enough to tell her one of my stories about Mama and Papa, and the Tweten antics.

I already had become known at the hospital as the storyteller, often entertaining my patients while I cared for them. As I told my isolation patient one of those stories, I soaked all her linens in a tub of diluted Lysol. In the morning I would wring out the sheets and place them in a special bag marked "SOILED LINEN" and send it to the laundry room.

45

I made certain my "mummy" patient was as comfortable as she could be and promised to come back and tell her another Tweten story before going off duty. As I stepped from her room, I faced a hall full of blinking lights – all calling for attention at the same time. I was alone on the floor now, except for periodic checks by the night supervisor. Where should I start?

When I saw old Zeb leaning over the fire escape rail, his open gown blowing in the breeze, I knew my first responsibility. He was cyanotic, his face etched against the street light.

"No, no, Mr. Zeb, you must not get out of bed!" I cried out.

"Had to get some air! Can't breathe in that danged tent; so I climbed out. I want to go home and sit on my porch and get some cool night air. It's too hot tonight!"

It was hot all right, and humid – Chicago in July. Carefully, I helped my cardiac patient back to bed and urged him to stay in the cool tent – a large canvas contraption, with only a peephole for the nurse to look inside. No wonder he wanted "out" to his porch.

When Mr. Zeb was settled, I ran to put saline packs on nineteen-year-old Bill's face.

His mother's eyes filled with fear as she watched her son's fever soar. More aspirin and liquids! I sponged him with cool water and urged his mother to force the liquids and keep sponging his hot body.

Across the hall Mrs. Olsen couldn't sleep so I warmed some milk for her and talked for a few minutes to reassure her that the long night would pass and by morning she would be better. I was trying to reassure both of us. The mustard plasters were bringing results and her pneumonia-filled lungs were relenting at last.

The elevator door closed and I heard the ambulance attendant announce, "Hey, Nursie, you have a new patient."

"Diagnosis?" I asked.

"Observation," he grinned.

Together we got her into bed and put the side rails up. The incoherent speech and jerking motions warned me of a long night with an advanced alcoholic.

I closed the fire escape, the only source of a breeze. The whir of small fans mingled with the snores. For a brief moment I wiped my perspiring face and stopped for a cracker and a cold drink of milk. Before I could finish the milk, my new patient started yelling about the rats in her room. There she stood, all two hundred pounds of her. With the open hospital gown in perpetual motion, she walked on her bed, bumping the side rails and yelling, "Get a broom to chase the rats!"

I ran to the phone. "Please send an intern — I can't handle her." Grabbing a broom I began to "chase rats" at my patient's direction.

"Over there!" she yelled. "Get that rat! You got him! Now get that one!"

I kept the broom in perpetual motion while my cheerleader waved me on with her flapping gown. Out of the corner of my eye I saw the interns in the hall, watching the performance, and nearly overcome with hysterics. That moved me to chase the interns with the broom.

Mercifully they calmed down long enough to push the needed hypodermic needle into the patient's exposed posterior. The sedative took effect and before long her snores joined the others. The interns spread the story that they weren't sure who the patient was that night.

One gentle intern, Dr. Gibbs, checked Grandma Olsen and saw that she was still awake. He warmed another cup of milk for her and sat beside her until she fell asleep, holding his hand. That memory stays on the backroads of my mind.

Four A.M. came too soon! The sound of bedpans and wash basins rattling on the cart was loud enough to wake the dead. Sleepy-eyed patients brushed their teeth and slurped pink mouthwash, while I washed other faces and hands. Some of them fell asleep on their bedpans. Grandpa drank his mouthwash.

There were urine samples to gather, insulin shots to give, temperatures to take, saline dressings to apply and the isolation case to care for. And there was Mr. Zeb and the fire escape!

A private duty night nurse had asked me to check on her patient while she went for a cup of coffee. "He's sound asleep, side rails are up, and I'm sure he'll sleep until I return."

The patient was another "observation" case—he had a history of delirium tremens.

When I settled Mr. Zeb again, I looked down the long dimly lit hall, and saw the private duty patient busily urinating in all the flower pots down the hallway.

"Glad I found the bathroom," he slurred, and

proceeded back to his room and climbed over the rail. I tucked him in and said, "Good night."

When his nurse returned he was sleeping peacefully and she said, "I'm glad he didn't give you any trouble."

"None at all," I answered. She never knew how the flowers got watered that night.

Sleepy-eyed patients brushed their teeth and slurped pink mouthwash. Grandpa Joe drank his.

Before dawn, it seemed that the long, hot shadows kept trying to close in on me like a heavy mantle. My eyes drooped. My legs ached. Wearily I reached for the chart to record temperatures and medicines. I turned at the sound of footsteps.

Coming down the hall in the early dawn was the familiar figure of Dr. Thornton with his Abe Lincoln appearance and a sack of oranges on his back. Unpressed clothes hung on his gaunt frame, but his keen eyes were filled with compassion and humor. "Just thought you might need a good orange to keep you awake for the day crew," he chuckled.

I hugged his stooped shoulders and kissed the cheek of our family's beloved physician. How often Mama had brought sick, suffering humanity to Dr. Thornton's office. His roll-top desk could never close and neither could his heart.

Without even glancing at the charts, he ambled

into his patients' rooms with his pocket full of blue and pink pills. "Now, Honey," he told Mrs. Olsen, "it's not so bad. You'll be home in no time."

Then disregarding isolation techniques, he pushed aside the gown and gloves—in order to visit the new isolation patient. "Foolishness, foolishness," he muttered, pushing the bandages aside. "Nothing like soap and water—good old soap and water."

"Now, now, young man," he said in Bill's room. "You look better already. A few more days and the infection will be gone. Reminds me of a story I heard on a fishing trip in Alaska . . . "

When Dr. Thornton left, pink and blue pills were on the bedside table and Bill was laughing. "I'll be back this evening—and it will all be all right," he told the boy. And I knew it would be!

I never found out what the blue and pink pills were, but they worked! With a chuckle, Dr. Thornton moved on to the other floors, his bag of oranges over his shoulder. He had come into my darkness and brought light.

7

HOME

Quietly she reminded me, "Your strength and help come from the Lord."

I rocked in Mama's rocking chair and watched her roll out pie crust for the Sunday dinner lemon pies. In the quiet of Mama's kitchen I drank in the peace of belonging and sipped a cup of coffee. This was my first weekend at home in many weeks but it was as though I had never been away. On Monday, after a month of night duty, I would begin the morning shift again, but tomorrow I would attend the regular Sunday morning service in Papa's church.

The long hours of night duty had left me weary and I fell asleep in Mama's rocker. When I awakened, I saw that Mama was looking at me anxiously. Quietly she reminded me, "Your strength and help come from the Lord. He will never fail you, Margaret." Her words filled my heart, and the familiarity of the room brought refreshing to my soul.

I knew from Grace that a lot of the family meals these days consisted of potatoes fried in lard. The depression days brought a number of people to seek food and shelter at Mama's table. But she declared stoutly, "I have never seen the righteous forsaken or His seed begging bread." For Mama, God's words were a fact of life.

Everything in the kitchen was in preparation for the next day. The homemade soup and freshly baked rye bread were for Saturday's supper but the meatballs and lemon pies were for Sunday's dinner.

I was home—and a part of the Saturday night ritual of shampoos and baths. Clean clothes were laid out for the morning and shoes were polished. The dining room table was set, potatoes peeled and carrots diced. Meatballs were ready for the frying pan; apple sauce cooled in a bowl.

When the younger children were finally tucked into bed, Mama and I closed the day with a cup of coffee and a sugar lump. For the special occasion of "Margaret is home," she managed day-old sweet rolls for a penny apiece. Life was good!

That night I was back in our bed—Doris in the middle, Grace by the wall. I took my place on the edge. We laughed and talked until sleep tucked us into a land of dreams.

Papa greeted the day with a rousing Norwegian hymn: "Early now on Sunday morning we lift our songs of praise to God." Nothing had changed in the Tweten home!

Mama's meatballs were sizzling in the frying pan. Hot coffee, toast and oatmeal waited as the Tweten clan emerged from the bedrooms.

I fell into the routine as though I had never been away — dishes done, beds made up, and everything in order before Sunday school.

Scrubbed and dressed in our best, we walked down Wrightwood Avenue to Logan Square. Papa strode ahead of us in striped trousers and swallowtailed coat, his coattails blowing in the wind.

Mama had happily nodded her approval when she checked his high starched collar and white shirt. There was no doubt about it. Papa was a handsome man!

The church family greeted me warmly and assured me of their love and prayers.

"Did you know that your father cried the first Sunday you were in training?" Leona chuckled delightedly. "He actually cried — and said, 'You must excuse me. This is the first Sunday Margaret hasn't been here in church.' "

"You mean, he *missed* me? I didn't think he knew I was gone!"

"Oh, he misses you. He just won't tell you. But I saw him cry. Your father loves you all very much — he just doesn't know how to show it."

I watched Papa in the pulpit, but I couldn't think of anything else. Papa missed me! He really missed me!

I was home!

At dinner we sat down at Mama's table covered with a starched linen cloth. The familiar menu of meatballs and all the trimmings blended with the stories from Barney and Leona who sat with us around the table.

When the table was cleared, Mama brought in her famous lemon pies and coffee. I knew that the potatoes fried in lard would come later — probably the rest of the week — but today was a time of feasting and joy.

"Oh, he misses you. He just won't tell you. But I saw him cry."

Papa dipped his sugar lump in his coffee and exclaimed, "Ja, Mama, that was the best pie you ever made." He always said that and we all always agreed.

Sunday afternoon was a time for naps or long walks. Night duty had exhausted me and I was ready for a nap. I had walked in the hospital corridors.

The house became quiet, the Sunday kind of stillness. Dishes were done, and Mama and the children were napping. Papa had gone into his study for his quiet time before the evening service and Barney, Leona and Grace went for a walk. I quickly fell asleep in my old room.

The next thing I knew, Mama had the coffee pot on. Leona and the others had returned from their walk and Papa came out of the study. It was time for afternoon coffee.

By five o'clock, we all marched down Wrightwood Avenue again to the Logan Square Church. It was time for B.Y.P.U. (our Baptist Young People's Union, but the ages ranged from 1 to 100—we were all young). After the various "youth groups" met, the Ruth Society served refreshments. We ate open-faced limpa bread sandwiches with goat cheese, hard-boiled eggs with anchovies, spiced cheese and mutton roll. Coffee cakes and gallons of coffee with thick cream were added— then the sugar lumps.

By 7:30 we had gathered for the evening service. The choir sang and the string band played, and then Papa preached.

At the close of the service, goodbyes were exchanged. At home I picked up my brown bag and Papa and I walked to the streetcar together. He read the Bible and I watched the city from the dusty window until we left the streetcar and walked through the doors of the Norwegian American Hospital.

I kissed Papa on the cheek and thanked him for bringing me safely back to the hospital. I knew that the extra five cents for carfare was a sacrifice.

I felt particularly blessed—I had a haven to go to when I was so exhausted. Many of the trainees I knew were from out of town and could not go home. Some didn't even have a home to go to. Being able to come home and get into the same familiar setting and the same routine was especially important to me. It had given me a needed sense of security. It restored my perspective, refreshed my sense of personal identity and renewed my strength.

8

THE OBSTETRICS DEPARTMENT

*Everyone rejoiced when the doctor held
up the wrinkled, yelling baby boy.*

I marvel at the plan of God
　That takes a seed from one—and then the other—
And breathes within the breath of life
　That makes one a Dad, and one a Mother.

This miracle—soft, fuzzy face,
　Clenched fists and wrinkled nose—
We stand guard around your place
　And wonder at ten tiny toes.

The world stands still, all cares forgotten—
　The past a dream, the future is here.
In this, our son, we have begotten,
　For perfect love casts away fear.

Around this circle, made of three,
　God enfolds us in His perfect love.
His Son He gave for you and me—
　His priceless gift from Heaven above.

No textbook could describe my sense of wonder as I watched the form of that living baby emerge from the entrance to his former home—his safe haven for nine months.

"I'm going to have a baby," had been the heartbeat of that young mother. Preparation and dreams followed the growth of the life within her. Then the magic moment arrived and the child entered a world of light and sound.

A baby's cry! Everyone rejoiced! I was awed, and thrilled beyond words when the doctor held up the wrinkled, yelling baby boy. "I never cease to marvel at the miracle of birth," he said as he handed the baby to me to wash and rub with warm oil.

I put a vaseline gauze dressing over the baby's navel and secured it with a belly band wrapped snugly. I could hardly breathe from excitement as I dressed the squirming infant in a soft triangle-shaped diaper, a warm shirt and a long flannel gown. I wrapped him in a blanket to keep him warm and to give him a sense of snug safety . . . that same safety and security he had felt such a little while before in his young mother's womb.

The mother was wheeled to her room and the baby was placed in a crib where the proud father watched his son through the nursery window; a blue name tag identified this matchless young heir.

Back on Fourth Floor Annex, nineteen-year-old Bill had died. I had wanted him to live but at that time there was no medication that could stop the infection which finally stole his life.

Old Mr. Zeb had climbed out of his tent for the last time.

The tall Polish policeman looked for me, saying, "I wanted to give a box of candy to the nurse who cared for my sister." Then he left the hospital to place flowers on his sister's grave.

Mrs. Goldstein was still yelling, "Help! I'm dying!" It looked as though she would live a long life. The cast was due to come off, but it remained to be seen whether she would walk or spend the rest of her days in a wheelchair.

Grandpa Joe finally got rid of that "danged contraption" and he was going home to his "own toilet."

As for me, I was on a happy floor where mothers nursed their babies and nurses told stories and doctors laughed.

I remembered the Swedish bricklayer who was in the waiting room and took him a cup of coffee. He sat rigidly on the edge of the seat, formally dressed in his black suit, white starched collar, and black derby hat, his feet squeezed into polished shoes. I held out the coffee but he just sat and waited.

Finally, Helga, his blue-eyed wife, was wheeled out of the delivery room. When the doctor spotted her husband, he announced, "Mr. Svenson, you have a fine son!"

With great dignity, Mr. Svenson doffed his hat, shook hands with his wife and said, "T'ank you, Mrs. Svenson." With that he went home, changed his clothes and went to work. He'd have to lay a lot of bricks in order to rear his newborn son.

Although the maternity wing was usually a happy place, there were occasional tragedies.

I was delighted that I could be relieved long enough to sing in the chorus. Was I in for a surprise!

When an older couple had their first child, a little girl with a spina bifida, we wept with them. Every day they came, hand in hand, to watch their special child in the nursery. When the baby finally could be cared for at home, they brought a satin quilt and a soft pillow for her enlarged head to rest on. Then they lovingly cared for their little one until she died a little more than a year later.

"We gave our baby so much love," they said when they returned to visit us. "And you can never give love without it comes back to you. We are richer for the love we gave."

One day an elderly doctor was delivering a baby when suddenly a look of horror crossed his face. He delivered a misshapen monstrosity.

"Oh, my God," he cried. "I delivered this mother and her sisters — and to think she gave birth to this. I can't even look at it!" He turned away, whipping off his mask, his face ashen.

The mother was anesthetized, blissfully unaware of the tragedy. A solemn quiet settled over the delivery room. No one moved. Unexpectedly, a soft breath escaped the misshapen form — and then total silence.

Without a word, a nurse placed a blanket over the still body.

The grief-stricken doctor slowly shook his head, and forced the order, "She must never know; I'll talk to her husband."

Like a tender father, the doctor stroked the young mother's hair, murmuring, "I'm sorry Betsy girl—so sorry, Honey." Turning to us, he added sadly, "In all my years of medicine, I have never seen anything like this." He looked older, defeated, when he walked out to see the husband.

I remembered the pain of this tragic delivery later when I rotated to Cook County Hospital and saw a four-year-old boy who barked like a dog and had fur on his chest and back. Experts came from everywhere to study this child, knowing that there are some things in life that are worse than death.

With all the agony of these deformities in life, and with all the ecstasy of a joyful birth, the maternity wing also has its comedy.

A year later, after training in many areas of nursing, I was back on night duty in the O. B. department. The nurses planned a Halloween party, and invited a number of outside guests.

In rare form, Miss Rosie asked Mr. Hartsmire to organize a nurses' chorus to sing for the party. They practiced for hours.

Mr. Hartsmire was tall and thin, and his favorite song was "The Lovely Amaryllis."

"Oh, Miss Rosendahl," he beamed during one of

the rehearsals, "you have a beautiful voice, and I can just see you tripping through the lovely amaryllis."

Miss Rosie, suddenly coy, blushed with pleasure and urged Mr. Hartsmire to sing for us. He persuaded her to join him. For a brief moment they were young again, tiptoeing through tulips and amaryllis.

No one at rehearsal dared smile; we were in awe. With a burst of enthusiasm, we joined the music and marched with them into the amaryllis.

At the party the nurses' chorus would watch Mr. Hartsmire direct them with his magic baton in one hand as he played the piano with the other. Then he would switch. Miss Rosie watched in awe!

I was to be on duty the night of the party, but was delighted that I could be relieved long enough to sing in the chorus. Was I in for a surprise!

Some weeks earlier, the O.B. intern who was to be on duty with me had gone on a banana diet. Bananas were scarce then so we saved as many as we could for him. One night we ate the inside of a banana and then carefully replaced the peel in perfect position.

We called Dr. W. "We found a banana!"

"I'll be right there!" He answered. He fell for our trick, but immediately suspected me, and vowed to get even.

Another night, while Dr. W was waiting for his chance, O.B. was too quiet so we nurses decided to bring some life into our department. We called Dr. W out of a sound sleep. "Hurry, we have a patient ready to deliver."

Sleepily, he scrubbed and slipped into the sterile gown I was holding for him. He pulled on his gloves and rushed to the delivery table. The patient was yelling!

Suddenly, the nurse with a pillow under her gown sat up. "Surprise!" we called. Once again, he was sure this innocent-looking preacher's kid was at the bottom of the affair. He vowed, "Tweetie — I'll get you one day!"

The night of the Halloween party I had a patient who wasn't in active labor yet. It was one of those rare nights when patient and nurses shared stories and laughter.

When Dr. W came up to check things, he had persuaded someone to grab me and hold me down, and he proceeded to paint a red mercurochrome mustache and goatee on my face. Suddenly, I was wearing a "Halloween mask," and everyone within sight rocked with laughter.

Then the phone rang! It was Miss Rosie, calling for Miss Tweten to join the chorus.

"Oh Miss Rosendahl," I stammered, "You know how much I enjoy singing in Mr. Hartsmire's chorus — especially 'The Lovely Amaryllis,' but you taught us that duty comes before pleasure."

My audience — standing close by me at the nurses' station — doubled up in laughter.

My honey-voiced words continued. "I must stay with my patient. She needs me, so please excuse me from the chorus."

Later, I found out that Miss Rosie had told Mr. Hartsmire, "That lovely Miss Tweten should be called the 'All-American Nurse.' I know how she loves to sing, but she wouldn't leave her patient."

Mr. Hartsmire assured Miss Rosie, "That's your wonderful training that sends the Florence Nightingales into the world."

I scrubbed with everything in sight but my red mustache left a blushing pink face. I guess Dr. W felt avenged because we were able to call a truce, and we remained good friends after that.

Later the nurses had their own day! Someone put croton oil (which acts like castor oil) in the fudge. With sweet smiles, the nurses presented the fudge at the intern's quarters. That night, all the interns were on twenty-four-hour duty!

9

TRAUMAS AND TRUST

I screamed again, "Hertha! There was a man in here!"
"Good," she answered. Then, suddenly awake, she screamed too.

I awoke out of a sound sleep, aware of a menacing form leaning over my bed. I froze — my face hidden in the shadows. At first I thought one of the interns had come into the wrong hall. But the street light revealed an intruder. I lay motionless and prayed.

My roommate, usually a light sleeper, was sound asleep that night.

Suddenly I jumped up and screamed, "Hertha!"

She rolled over in her bed and answered, "That's all right Margaret. I know all about it." She had been dreaming! The intruder fled out of the room and down the fire escape. Apparently a latecomer had left it un-

64

locked, after Miss Abrahamson's nightly check.

I screamed again! "Hertha! There was a man in here."

"Good," she answered. Then suddenly awake, she screamed, too!

We ran down the long hall to make a report to the telephone operator.

Within moments, Miss Rosie appeared, with curlers in her hair and dressed in a big bathrobe. Other supervisors came as well. Seconds later, several interns and externs were on the scene, and finally, the Chicago police arrived.

Hertha and I were still shaking. "Now, now, Miss Tweten," the director of nurses said accusingly, "Are you sure it wasn't your boyfriend, Harold, sneaking up the fire escape?" Miss Rosie glared at me.

One policeman offered his suggestion. "I know there's a tall young man who stands under this window to say good-night." He smiled directly at me!

"That is my friend, Harold Jensen," I blushed. "Harold always waits to see if I get to my room safely." They all smiled—except Miss Rosie.

The police sent the interns to search the empty rooms and to check the bathrooms.

Miss Rosie stood motionless, arms folded, glowering at me. I shuddered. I was sure she'd call Papa and he would somehow blame me for all this commotion.

Hertha and I huddled together. When everything was clear, the police wrote up the incident and promised to guard the dormitory area. Everyone left except one young extern.

"Don't go," Hertha pleaded, "I have to go to the bathroom, and you are coming with me with that flashlight." The doctor obliged and flashed his light into the bathroom, then gave Hertha an "all clear."

"Margaret, you might as well go now, too, while I'm here on guard," he offered. I was too embarrassed and said, "Oh, no. I don't have to go."

The five brothers turned to me with a helpless, desperate look. "She's our baby sister," one of them said. "She's only nineteen."

The extern disappeared with his flashlight—and suddenly I had to go to the bathroom. It seemed that the long hall had no end, and the empty stalls looked threatening. Hertha stood in the doorway of our room and called out her encouragement. I came back safely and we finally got to bed, but not until Hertha checked the fire escape door and then locked our door. She piled up chairs and moved a desk in front of the door. No one would ever enter that door again uninvited!

The interns teased me saying, "The preacher's daughter had night visitors." I tried to laugh with them, but for years the fear could be tempered only by my stubborn trust in God.

One day—long after the night visitor—Hertha walked into the room. I was packing my brown box.

"What in the world are you doing?" She asked.

"I gave the wrong medicine," I sobbed. "And Miss Rosie said if we ever, but ever, gave the wrong medicine we might as well start packing."

"What did you give?"

"I gave milk of magnesia instead of cascara. The patient had been on cascara before and I didn't see the change. Oh, I don't know what to do."

"Does Miss Hanna know?"

"Of course. I told her right away. She said that we could not afford to make errors, even small ones. Someday it could be fatal." I kept packing.

"Telephone for Tweetie," someone called out.

I just knew it was Miss Rosie! I could hear her now . . . but it was Miss Hanna. I was to report back to Fourth Floor.

"Miss Tweten, you are a good nurse," Miss Hanna said, her expression almost kindly. "But sometimes you try too hard. You do more than you should, and you try to protect those who don't carry out their duties. Now, I want you to remember that you can't be responsible for everyone. You do your work, and I will see to it that the others do their share. I just wanted you to know that I think you are becoming a fine nurse."

"But, Miss Hanna, what about the medicine? I told you I gave milk of magnesia instead of cascara."

"Oh, yes . . . I talked to the doctor, and he said that he was putting the patient back on cascara. The milk of magnesia was ineffective. I am sure you will never give a wrong medicine again—if you carefully

67

read the orders *each time*. Take nothing for granted, Miss Tweten. You must *check* your orders. Now get to class."

"Thank you, Miss Hanna. Oh, I do thank you." I started to reach out to hug her, but drew back. "I want to be a good nurse," I whispered.

I was surprised to see a tenderness in her eyes, a haunting longing. Many years later I learned that she had loved, "not wisely, but too well."

I thanked God for His boundless grace, and I unpacked my box. Hertha and I went to class. I never again forgot to check my medicines *three times* in accordance with Miss Hanna's rules.

On another day, when exams were coming, Hertha and I sat on the fire escape stairs at dawn. We were memorizing our notes from Dr. G's Materia Medica. The sun rose over the skyscrapers of Chicago, and down on the streets, we heard the welcome sound of horses pulling their milk wagons. The rattle of the bottles heralded the entrance of the new day.

Before long, we were pinning on our long white starched pinafores and fastening our caps in place, ready to march in order to chapel. This time we led the line, and the capless probies brought up the rear.

When I reported for duty later that day, I saw five tall men pacing the hall, their fists clenched in anger. Their weatherbeaten faces and large rough hands told me they were farmers. They looked miserable in their Sunday clothes and polished shoes.

"What's wrong?" I asked the night nurse.

"A beautiful girl is dying in that room, apparently from an induced abortion. You're assigned to her."

Deep within me I felt a new respect for God's protective laws.

I walked into the room with a basin of water to bathe my new patient, and caught my first glimpse of the dying girl. Black curls clung to her forehead; her body was feverish, and her eyes were glassy.

The five brothers followed me into the girl's room. "Please, Sis," they said to her, "tell us who he is. Please!"

They turned to me with a helpless, desperate look.

"She's our baby sister," one of them said. "She's only nineteen. She came to visit our aunt who took her to the ballroom to see how exciting Chicago is compared to the farm back home. Some man at the ballroom sweet-talked her, and no one knew about it until our aunt found her bleeding. She called the ambulance."

"Now Sis won't talk to us," the older brother added. "Mama and Papa don't speak English and have never been off the farm — so we had to come. Poor Papa, he's left with all the chores." He shook his head.

"If only Sis would tell us who . . . we'd kill the guy. We owe her that much. She's Mama's baby girl."

I ushered the five brothers back into the hall and the pacing with clenched fists began again. I went back into the room, and quickly bathed the girl. As I cared for her, I prayed for her. "Oh God, she's so young!" I said. She was nineteen . . . and so was I!

She died quietly that day and the nurses wept openly with the grief-stricken brothers. One brother spoke through taut lips, "Now we must tell Mama and Papa our sister is gone. She never told us who he was."

I watched them walk slowly out like bent, old men. Their grief was too deep for words.

That night I read in my Bible:

> Forever, O LORD, thy word is settled in heaven.
> Thy word is a lamp unto my feet and a light unto my path.
> Thou art my hiding place and my shield: I hope in thy word.
> Order my steps in thy word: and let not any iniquity have dominion over me.
> (Psalm 119:89,105,114,133)

I kept thinking about Papa's sermon on "The wages of sin is death; but the gift of God is eternal life" (Romans 6:23). Deep within me I felt a new respect for God's protective laws. I also experienced a sense of awe at the consequences of taking God's laws lightly! I wondered how many people suffer as a result of disobedience to God. Where had this girl gone wrong? When she left the farm for Chicago? When she went to the ballroom with her aunt? When she yielded to the sweet talk of a stranger? When she tried to rid her body of an unborn child? Or was she solely the victim of a man bent on sin?

Even if Papa was unreasonably strict with us Twetens, I sensed a new security in the admonition: "Honour thy father and mother" (Ephesians 6:2).

"But Mama," I used to say, "Papa is always so unreasonable."

"Ja, ja. Who doesn't know that? But I don't read in my Bible anywhere, 'Honour your father when he is reasonable.' " She would smile patiently. "Now, if Papa is unreasonable, he will answer to God. But if you don't honor Papa, who do you want to answer to?"

"But, Mama, you mix it up."

"No, you mix it up. The Word of God is very plain. It is very simple—just not so easy to do."

I thought about the five brothers going home to tell their mama and papa that their sister was dead. Suddenly I could hardly wait until time to go home tomorrow—just to be at the table, to feel the security and love of a family. It was true Papa was stubborn and unreasonable at times, but obeying him brought a sense of security. We can trust God's laws—they bring order. Man's laws, without God's order, bring confusion.

In spite of what had happened, I fell asleep in a settled peace that night, thinking, *The LORD shall preserve thy going out, Margaret Tweten, and thy coming in* (Psalm 121:8).

10

TRIALS AND TRIUMPHS

The five "typhoid fever children" had been found alone, deserted by their parents — and were covered with lice.

From my tenth floor room in the nurses dorm, I looked out over Cook County Hospital, a massive complex of brick and stone, a medical city within a city. Far below me, the roar of Chicago's elevated trains, clanging street cars and automobile traffic mingled with the wailing siren of ambulances and police cars.

I was one of many student-affiliates at Cook County Hospital for six months' special training in pediatrics and contagious diseases. These nursing specialties were lacking in the smaller, private hospitals.

I wondered if I would ever find my way around this vast expanse of buildings as I headed for pediatrics, but I needn't have worried. When I entered the building, I met my supervisor, Mrs. Schroeder, a calm, quiet, self-assured woman whose very bearing said, "Everything is in control."

During a children's feeding period on pediatric rotation, I met Gladys Thompson, a student from Lutheran Deaconess Hospital. A warm, lasting friendship developed from that casual meeting. Looking back now, I know it was part of a divine plan!

Gladys and I worked together on the tuberculosis ward. We moved cribs and beds out to the roof garden where the patients could see skyscrapers etched against the high, smoke-filled sky and benefit from the sun as it filtered bravely through the haze. We fed the children between-meal snacks and read to them, and then we settled them down for extra naps. Rest, food, fresh air and love was the prescription for these fragile children.

On another floor — far from the garden-roof — I donned gown, mask and gloves to irrigate pus-filled eyes and to cleanse open sores — caused by venereal disease. This encounter with the wages of sin was particularly trying for me, this fresh, agonizing realization of how the innocent suffer. I knew from childhood that blessings flow from generation to generation; but here on the pediatric wing, I learned how the destructive wages of sin also pass from generation to generation.

One nurse wanted to adopt a beautiful child who had been abandoned by her parents. But the child tested positive for syphilis and gonorrhea. The nurse wept — her dream of adoption shattered — but she continued to buy clothes and toys for that lonely child.

One day a policeman brought five children from

the same family into the pediatric admitting room. Their bodies and hair were soiled with feces and vomitus. Diagnosis: "typhoid fever." They had been found alone, deserted by their parents—and were covered with lice.

Impulsively, the child pulled my mask down and kissed me on the mouth.

One by one, I bathed them on a porcelain slab, using a shower type hose, a soft brush and lysol soap. After their heads were shaved, I scrubbed them with a cleansing solution and wrapped their heads in towels. They sat in a row, silent and terrified—clean now in white hospital gowns and wrapped in warm blankets, their faces still pale. Their haunting, solemn eyes followed my every move as I tried to get them to sip some weak tea. We nurses adopted them and showered them with love until the smiles came and the hair grew back. Through the years I have wondered what happened to those frightened children who had to learn about love from strangers in white.

The contagious wards never had enough beds. During the years of the polio epidemic, disease victims filled every available space. Tragedy and heartbreak surrounded us. Bodies were crippled for life.. Some children would never walk again—others would never grow old. Diphtheria patients cried in fear; scarlet fever patients filled many cribs. Even one of the interns died.

One day, as I finished bathing a beautiful child who had a high fever and rash, she impulsively pulled my mask down and kissed me on the mouth. Her arms wound around my neck, and she clung to me, begging to be held. I desperately tried to replace my mask.

"I love you," she whispered.

When the long day drew to a close, a deep weariness settled over me. It was difficult enough to care for adults who were ill, but my encounter with wards of sick children seemed unending.

Tomorrow I was going home — home to Mama's kitchen, to health and cleanliness, where simplicity and order were a way of life. I prayed for the wisdom to be thankful for the simple things — home, family, a warm fire, a loaf of homemade bread and a cup of coffee.

The next day when the Fullerton Avenue streetcar stopped, I stepped off and trudged heavily to the flat on Ridgeway Avenue, arriving just in time for Mama's afternoon coffee. To think I could spend the night and have all the next day, too!

The kitchen was warm and the hot liquid was delicious, but I couldn't swallow much of the coffee cake. My head ached, and I dozed in the rocking chair.

I awoke, and realized that I had to go back to the hospital. I longed to stay home, but the way I was feeling, I had to report to the infirmary in case I couldn't return to work. The rules were strict. Mama looked anxious as she secured my scarf and whispered, "I'll pray." Her comforting words rang in my ears.

Papa walked with me to the street car. I shivered in the cold. "Ja, Margaret," he said tenderly, "we will get you to the infirmary and perhaps you can return home tomorrow." On the streetcar he tried to read. I kept shivering. When we reached the infirmary, Papa said, "Good night," and I was admitted. We were both sure that a good night's sleep would be the cure.

I tried to focus on Harold. So young. So strong. "You have been very sick," he said.

Two nights later, I opened my eyes and saw the white face of my father staring intently at me, with a look I remembered from many years ago.

I was three years old then—standing behind a glass cubicle in the New York contagious hospital. I had diphtheria. I reached out my childish arms to be held, but the glass partition separated us. I remember just standing there—not crying—as I watched Papa's sad white face through the glass.

The memory blurred! I was no longer a child, but I saw him again looking at me with that sad, white face. Mama stood beside Papa, looking anxiously at me—and Harold Jensen, my friend from the Northern Baptist Seminary, was with them. Why were they there?

"We are praying for you, Margaret. You will be fine." Mama's words seemed far away.

I tried to focus on Harold. So young. So strong. His lips moved. "You have been very sick. The hospital called your parents and I brought them over," he said. "We've been here all night, but, Margaret, you are going to be well." Harold seemed far away, too.

Faces and sounds blurred again: "A strep throat— temperature of 105" . . . "Didn't think she'd make it

. . . " Papa's white face . . . Mama's tear-filled eyes
. . . Harold's worried expression . . .

I remembered the nineteen-year-old boy who had died from an infected tooth. Then I remembered the child, the one with scarlet fever, who had pulled my isolation mask from my face and then kissed me. My thoughts slowed and stopped, and I fell asleep.

Our six-month rotation training was almost finished so when my infection was gone, I returned to our infirmary at Norwegian American Hospital.

Miss Rosie thought I could be up and going, but our old family physician, Dr. Thornton, said, "Not on your life. This child needs rest. She has been very sick."

He winked at me as Miss Rosendahl walked stiffly away in her starched uniform. He left his blue and pink pills, told me fish stories from Alaska, and promised oranges and grapefruit in the morning. "You'll be fine," he called back as he lumbered down the hall.

He was right! He usually was.

It wasn't long then before graduation day came, and so did State Board examinations. Thanks to Dr. G and his tough rules, we made high grades in Materia Medica. My lowest score was in dietetics. I had boiled oysters in milk for an hour to prepare oyster stew. No one let me forget that one!

On graduation night, Miss Rosie was in her glory! So was Papa! Papa gave the invocation, and in glowing terms thanked Miss Rosendahl for her contribution to society.

Mr. Hartsmire tiptoed through the tulips and led

us to the lovely amaryllis. He waved his baton as though we were the St. Olav's chorus. Life was beautiful!

We stood in shining white, from starched caps to polished shoes. Our striped uniforms and black cotton stockings were packed away. Forever. A shiny gold pin held the memorable date: *N.A.H.T.S. 1937* (Norwegian American Hospital Training School).

He looked at Mama and said, "I thought, If that young girl can smile, I can't be dying *— so I determined to live to see her smile again."*

After the graduation ceremonies came a reception for families and friends. Papa and Mama enjoyed the event to the fullest, especially the stories from former patients. There were many, like the Polish policeman, who remembered. And came!

Mama was deeply moved when an elderly doctor made a great effort to attend the ceremonies, defying his own doctor's orders.

"I had to come," he insisted. Turning to Mama, he added, "I remember the day I came to the hospital with a serious heart attack. When I was placed in the canvas oxygen tent I knew I was dying. But this child," he turned to me, "put her head in the tent and smiled at me. 'You are going to be all right,' she told me. 'I'll take good care of you.'" He looked back at Mama. "I thought, *If that young girl can smile, I can't be dying* — so I determined to live to see her smile again." I kissed his wrinkled cheek, and thanked him for coming.

After graduation, Gladys Thompson, my friend from Cook County Hospital, and I worked together at Lutheran Deaconess Hospital. Life was still beautiful— but it was changing.

Floor duty hours had dropped from twelve a day to eight. After duty I changed into street clothes since rules forbade uniforms outside the hospital. I still wore the brown coat from Mrs. Knight.

I saved every dollar I earned, eager to repay the $300 cash Mama had drawn from an insurance policy to buy my books and uniforms when I entered training.

Soon Papa no longer shook the stove at 5 A.M. in the cold water flat on Ridgeway Avenue. The flat was empty. Grace and I watched the train leave for New York where Papa was to pastor Norwegian Baptist Church in Brooklyn. Then Grace left—to work in New York.

I was alone, yet not really alone because Harold Jensen and I were planning our wedding for June, 1938.

After our wedding in Brooklyn, we settled into a cozy apartment on Central Park Avenue in Chicago. Harold still attended Northern Baptist Seminary and I worked at Lutheran Deaconess Hospital. Life was really beautiful then.

11

THE HOMECOMING

I cringed at the way Kathryn barked, "Come down." It was exactly the way I had said it.

While the other grandchildren compete in games, six-year-old Kathryn bounces and skips through life — and, like her grandmother, tells stories.

I decided to take advantage of a half-price sale at Belk's department store, and I took Kathryn with me. It was early in the day and the store was quiet. Kathryn saw her opportunity, and asked the clerk, "Would you like to hear a story?" First thing I knew, she was well into a story about her Aunt Janice. The clerks listened and smiled as Kathryn said, "Well, one day when my Aunt Janice was a very little girl, she climbed high up in the cherry tree. She was hiding up there and eating the top ripe cherries. My Grammy kept looking and looking for her. All the neighbors were looking. Then

80

Papa said, 'We will have to call the police.'"

Kathryn was doing a good imitation of both Janice and me.

" 'You come right down,' Grammy said." (I cringed at the way Kathryn barked, "Come down" — because she was right. It was exactly the way I had said it.)

" 'Promise not to spank me!' " Kathryn went on, repeating the cry Janice had made.

" 'Come right down!' " (Me again.)

" 'Promise?' " (How could Kathryn sound so much like Janice?)

"All the neighbors said, 'Oh, Honey, you can come on down. Of course your mommy won't spank you.' " Kathryn sighed. "And Aunt Janice came down, and Grammy couldn't spank her." Her audience clapped enthusiastically!

It was time for us to leave!

With a smile and a happy skip, Kathryn called back, "I'll tell some more stories next time."

Later, when all the family was around the table (and not to be outdone by my granddaughter), I said, "Let me tell you a story about *The Homecoming.*"

"Is it true, Grammy?"

Our children want true stories! Maybe I've spoiled them. Sometimes I change the names and places, but my stories are true.

"It happened when I was nursing a patient who suffered from depression. She was even more upset because we couldn't get a private room for her . . . "

A new patient—a very old lady—was admitted to the other bed, and we pulled the curtain for privacy.

"It's all my fault. It's all my fault," moaned Ellie Mae. All the old lady's family members were there. "She was sleepin' when I went to make coffee, and the next thing I knew Granny was on the floor. Didn't hear no bump. She just lay thar so still. Lordy, I done thought she was gone for sure."

"Hush, Ellie Mae," comforted an aunt. "You done the best you could . . . and you called the Rescue Squad. Now hush, child!"

Granny, ninety, more or less, lay quietly on the white hospital bed, the glucose dripping into her bony arm. I checked her blood pressure and mumbled, "It's OK." And then I said, "The intern is on his way to get the family history."

By this time, Granny, wrinkled like a tree branch, her wispy hair tied in a knot on top of her head, was surrounded by her thirteen children. The fourteenth child, Willie, was on his way from a sawmill in Georgia. Three country preachers arrived and joined the family. Ellie Mae still sniffled into her Kleenex.

One preacher reminded everyone how much Granny loved the church homecoming with dinner on the grounds.

Zelda, the eldest daughter added, "Remember? We put Granny on a chair under the oak tree. She was all dressed up with her new straw hat. She said, 'I'm too tired to go around that table like you young 'uns, so go fetch Granny a little bite of each.'"

Everyone remembered how plate after plate had

made its way to Granny's lap, how she sampled each one and made comments about the cooks: "The strawberry puddin's about as good as mine," she chuckled. "Bettis knows how to cure a ham . . . Mary Jo's pickles not spicy enough, but good, mind you."

"Do tell, Ellie Mae, these folks believe in signs."

Granny apparently held court while all the kin paid homage, that is, all but Willie. "He took hisself off to Georgee and no doubt will end on the road gang. Rocky Creek is home, and folks don't need to go off with folks they ain't no kin to."

Then young B.J. reminded them how Granny was honored on Mother's Day, with the largest family. Everybody was there, that is, everybody but Willie.

"Stop that snifflin', Ellie Mae," one preacher admonished. "It's the Lord's will, that's what, and we can't argue with the Lord's will. Her time has come. What a pity, just before Homecoming. But you can be sure, it will be the biggest funeral in Rocky Creek county."

To all the family's anxious questions, I answered, "She's about the same—not responding, but her vital signs are stable."

"Do tell, Ellie Mae, these folks believe in signs. I told you to pay attention to Granny's signs." Zelda's voice was accusing. "She knowed her signs for plantin' and for deaths. Cain't see for the life of me how thet water in her arm does any good. Aunt Minnie got a cure that would put Granny on her feet in no time. I remember the day old B.J. fell . . . ”

On the other side of the curtain, the depressed patient was listening intently.

For a few moments, the family ran out of memories. No one spoke. Then the quiet was broken by the sound of clumsy footsteps as a wide-eyed young man stumbled into the room. He leaned low over Granny's bedside.

“Momma, Momma, Momma, it's Willie, your baby boy. Oh, Momma, Momma, tell me that you love me.”

Willie held one wrinkled hand in both of his and kissed her cheek. She seemed to wince, but just for a moment. “Oh, Lord—Momma, Ah done come home. Now speak to me,” he pleaded.

I tried to quiet him, but he yelled, “Ah has to know she loves me.” His glassy eyes were pleading.

“Just sit by her bed and tell her you love her,” I said as kindly as I could.

“Oh, Momma, Momma, Ah love you. If you love me, Momma, please . . . squeeze mah finger.” With a yell, he hollered, “She done squeezed mah finger, nurse. Momma loves me! She loves me!”

An attendant led Willie to the visiting room—and a cup of coffee. On the other side of the curtain, the depressed patient almost smiled.

“Now, Ma'am, I need some family history,” the intern said as he pushed his way to Granny's bedside.

“Oh, Lord, Doc. Momma lived here all her life,”

Zelda told him. "We all knows her history."

"Yes sir," the others added. "These preachers all know, too." The three preachers nodded in agreement.

The intern's face was expressionless. "How many children?"

"Fourteen, yes sir, all live in Rocky Creek. Momma saw to that — all but Willie. Ah reckon Willie better go home, Doc. You see, he didn't get to Homecoming last year, and his conscience is a hurtin'. It orter too! No one misses Homecoming in Momma's family."

"Does she drink or smoke?" the intern asked flatly, his eyes down.

Zelda drew up her shoulders and folded her arms, glaring at the intern. "Momma drink? No, siree, sir. Momma don't drink. A good Christian woman, she is, and nairy a drop in the house. Now Paw, it was heard to tell, had a still on the back forty, but Momma never knew."

The intern seemed slightly annoyed. "Does she smoke?" he droned on.

"You mean smoke them cigarettes, Doc? No fancy cigarettes for Momma." Zelda frowned. "Snuffin' she liked tolerable well. Right good corn Paw had . . . Momma healthy? Got kicked by a mule oncet, and stun'd by a bee."

Granny lay still as her history unfolded. Zeb, the oldest son, wiped his eyes as he listened to the conversation.

Young Zeke, one of the grandsons, was telling the other children how Granny watched *Medical Center* on

TV. "Granny would get excited and clap her hands when the ambulance raced through the big city streets. Just like Paw used to do," he chuckled. "That ambulance scats them cars like Paw did the chickens when he rode Nellie. Whee, they flew every which way. All them nice people in them white coats totin' that poor soul on that log . . . she gits to sleep on sheets she didn't wash . . . looks like Homecoming—folks all gatherin' round. Meet lots of new folks that-a-way.

"Granny's in a coma, and can't hear nuthin'." They talked on and on—until Willie returned.

"It was the ambulance ride she always clapped her hands for," young Zeke continued. "Every time *Medical Center* came on TV, Granny would say, 'Wheee—hear that sireen, Zeke?' "

Granny's wrinkled face looked so peaceful. The glucose continued to drip into her arm as the kin from Rocky Creek kept watch. "Granny's in a coma," they'd announce to each newcomer, "and can't hear nuthin'." They talked on and on, that is until Willie returned.

"Momma, Momma, it's Willie, your baby boy!" he cried. "Ah quit mah job at the mill, Momma. Made enough to git me a brand new truck. Ah'm comin' home to do loggin' in Rocky Creek . . . "

Suddenly Granny sat straight up. "Take me home, Willie, in that new truck!" The voice was frail, but the command was unmistakable.

"A miracle!" Ellie Mae cried. "It's a miracle!" Everyone talked at once. The preachers all had prayer, and Granny's kin went home. I was not at all surprised to hear the depressed patient, on the other side of the curtain, laugh out loud.

Granny was wheeled past the emergency room to the discharge center. She waved her bony hand. "I thank you nice folks. Y'all come see me, hear? It was nice to sleep in sheets I didn't wash. But the sireen was the best." She left behind a vision of a toothless smile in a wrinkled face, wrinkled like oak bark, and strong. The wispy knot on her head bobbed precariously as she was lifted into Willie's new truck. He tucked her hand-knit shawl around her shoulders and they were off.

The following Sunday, the folk from Rocky Creek stood to sing the closing hymn:

> Coming home, coming home;
> Never more to roam.
> Open wide thine arms of love;
> Lord, I'm coming home.

Willie had come back for Homecoming.

12

LOVE STORIES

The world stood still while doctors, nurses and cleaning staff prayed for one small child.

One of my favorite places is the ocean, especially when I'm there with my grandchildren. With an eye for beauty, my grandsons were watching Heather and her friend, Kris, jog on the beach.

"Heather wants to be a doctor," Chad said proudly of his sister.

"Wow!" Eric gave a long, low whistle.

Shawn's answer was equally as expressive. "Hey, she could be anything—writer, lawyer, doctor, or . . . a model!"

"So could you boys," I interjected, my hand firmly on Chad's shoulder. "Chad, you won first place in an art contest. Besides, you're a good soccer player, *and* a writer!"

Eric grinned. "Looks like you have some competition, Grammy!" With a quick hug, Eric joined the others and they ran down the beach, the rest of their remarks lost in the wind.

I found myself watching the children — and talking to myself. "Oh, you beautiful children, each of you is so different with a unique creative talent from God. Keep thankful hearts — remember, every perfect gift comes from above." My words raced on the wind behind them to the water's edge.

The ocean waves rolled over the sand. Fishermen were bringing in their boats. I found myself humming an old song:

> Shrimp boats are a-comin . . .
> Gotta hurry, hurry home . . .

I did. It was supper time!

Having all the family together during these sunny days was a gift from God. I thought of my grandchildren growing up and being able to go into various fields of work armed with wonderful new technology. I remembered a long ago time, and our lack of modern medicine, and when the prescription of love and prayer sometimes overcame that lack.

I was a young R.N. and had been assigned to a four-year-old girl who was fighting for her life. Diagnosis: ruptured appendix, peritonitis. The dressings on her enlarged abdomen had become saturated with purulent drainage.

She was the youngest of a large, devoted family

who all called themselves the "Knights of the Round Table." Each child had been given a knight's name in addition to his or her real name. The eldest was called Sir Dependability, another Sir Sincerity, a third Sir Kindness . . . this young girl was named Sir Love.

Sir Love's anxious parents took turns at the bedside of their beautiful, dying child.

The slow drip from a proctoclysis can sent fluid into her rectum. Needles under her skin sent fluid into the thighs from the hypodermoclysis method. Aspirin and cool sponging helped to lower her high temperature caused by the severe infection.

I gagged inwardly when I changed the abdominal dressings. Nevertheless, I smiled and told stories to Sir Love and to her parents as well. Stories about the Tweten family. Stories about Jesus.

Sir Love named me Miss Tweedledeedee. "Come, change my dressing real fast, Miss Tweedledeedee," she would call. She wanted to get it over with.

Whenever her doctor, a tall gentle man, came, he held back his tears and handed her a lollipop "Try to suck this, Sir Love," he would say. "You need the glucose."

One day she was too weak to suck the lollipop.

When I reached the hospital the next morning, the cleaning maids were huddled close together in the hall, crying.

"What happened?" I asked.

"Sister told me not to clean her room, not to disturb the family, because Sir Love is almost gone."

For a moment, the world stood still while doctors, Deaconess nurses and the cleaning staff prayed for one small child. Then I went into the room to change the dressings and sponge Sir Love. Her body was cyanotic. My heart ached. Her parents held hands and quietly prayed.

The men attending the conference looked up when the door opened, and they saw Wonder Boy, searching the faces around the table.

Day turned into night. Sir Love was still alive. I said good-bye to the parents and left.

In the morning, Sir Love was still alive. The cleaning woman cleaned the room. I bathed Sir Love and changed her dressings.

Her doctor came with a lollipop, and she sucked it. We dripped water into her mouth, and she swallowed. Color crept back into her face. Shouts of joy spread through every department of the hospital. Sir Love was alive!

Gradually she began to eat the special dishes the kitchen staff prepared. One day I took her in a wheelchair to visit the people who had wept and prayed and showered her with their love.

Months later, I was a guest in the home of the "Knights of the Round Table." Sir Love came in from the street where she had been riding her tricycle. Her grubby arms flew around my neck and I was smothered with sticky lollipop kisses. "Miss Tweedledeedee! You came!"

I smiled, remembering Sir Love. Perhaps one of my grandchildren would become a doctor. They would never have to administer lollipops for glucose and there would be miracle drugs to treat infections. But, even with all the modern technology, the power of love and prayer still tips the scales.

Another four-year-old child, the youngest of thirteen, fell into a washtub of scalding water. The entire family came to the Emergency Room with him. No one expected the child to live.

I recall holding him — he was swathed in gauze with only his eyes visible, peeping through the mask of bandages. Intravenous fluids dripped into his small veins.

He became the hospital pet, surrounded by love from every department. Dr. Al was his doctor. Usually brusque in his manner, Dr. Al, we knew, was a teddy bear — especially where children were concerned.

Under Dr. Al's care, "Wonder Boy" slowly improved, and eventually he was given the freedom to roam the hospital halls.

He visited nurses and patients, but Dr. Al was the one our bright-eyed Wonder Boy loved. He even followed him on rounds and called him "My Dr. Al."

One day there was a medical meeting in the conference room. Wonder Boy was roaming the halls and happened upon the door to the conference room.

The men attending the meeting looked up when

the door opened, and saw Wonder Boy, in his little hospital gown, searching the faces around the table. Suddenly his eyes lit up. "There he is, *My Dr. Al!*" The little boy ran to the doctor, and love had a shining moment in that conference room.

Love had its way again some years later when I was on a private duty case. My patient was in a coma, critical. There seemed to be little hope for recovery. But, just as I always did, I spoke softly to him, and assured him he would be better in the morning.

I told him what I was doing for him, saying such things as, "I'm changing your I.V."; or, "I have to turn you now." In between, I repeated Scripture verses of encouragement, verses like: "Fear thou not; for I am with thee: be not dismayed, for I am thy God: I will strengthen thee; yea, I will help thee; yea, I will uphold thee with the right hand of my righteousness" (Isaiah 41:10, KJV).

One day my comatose patient opened his eyes. "Mary. You must be Mary."

"No — but you are close. It is Margaret."

"I heard you; I heard your voice. You sound just like Mary."

Later, his story came in pieces. Mary was an army nurse he had loved, but both their parents rejected their idea of marriage because of religious differences.

"I loved her," he said softly. "We parted, but I never forgot her. I had made plans to find her — then I became ill. I need to find my Mary."

I waited, then answered quietly. "I have watched

your lovely wife sitting here day after day. I know devotion when I see it, and believe me, that kind is rare." I patted his hand. "You must not allow a dream from the past to cloud what you have in the present. You have been a gravely ill man, but your health is being restored. You must trust God to take care of your Mary. By coming into her life at this time, you could destroy both her and her family if she has one. Then what about the one who loves you now? Why don't you close the door to the past and give yourself to the present?"

Slowly he recovered enough to go home. Before he left he turned to me and said softly, "Thank you, *Mary* — thank you for everything."

Many months later I met his lovely wife again.

"Oh, I'm so glad to see you. My husband is a changed man since his illness. He decided to go to church with me and it is as though we are newlyweds. He used to be so quiet but our lives are so full these days. Strange what a serious illness can do! I guess coming close to death made him realize how precious life can be. I'll tell him I saw you."

A thankful heart stores up past mercies to feed faith in dark days. I heard that someplace — I think I'll try to remember it.

My romantic roommate was always in love with someone or something. When the soft music of "Speak to Me of Love" came on the radio, someone shouted down the hall, "They're playing your song, Hertha!" Then all the dormitory radios were turned up together for Hertha.

We teased Hertha about her "chicken farmer"

whom no one had met. But then she met Thor, and they lived happily ever after. Her song is still *her* song.

One day, I met a real chicken farmer, not in a romantic setting, but in the hospital.

"Cain't run no chicken farm without my woman."

He stood in the corridor, outside the door where his wife lay in a coma. His weathered face reflected the sun and wind; his thumbs nervously pulled at his over-all straps.

"Proud to meet you," he answered politely when I told him I was the morning nurse. Then he nodded toward his wife's room. "My woman's in that . . . " His voice choked up. "Cain't run no chicken farm without her."

I assured him that we would all take good care of her. The patient's room was quiet; the intravenous fluid dripped slowly into her veins. The doctor warned us not to move her, due to an embolism (an obstruction in a blood vessel). Constant care was needed to monitor medication and vital signs. She was cold and clammy.

One day I asked the doctor if we could lift her so I could put a warm blanket under her. Reluctantly, he agreed, "Only if four of you nurses lift her carefully." We did! I placed a warm blanket under her.

I talked to her quietly, cared for her, held her hand and quoted the 23rd Psalm. There was no response.

Her husband came to see her early each morning; then returned home to care for his chickens and twelve children. The eldest daughter, eighteen and newly married, helped care for the family.

One morning the farmer met me in the hall as he was leaving. "I got a pot of coffee perkin' in the room. Just had to do somethin' and I saw how all you nurses drink coffee. Just had to do somethin'."

I thanked him and took a cup. He smiled, then returned home to care for his chickens and children. Each morning it was the same routine. He was waiting for me with a cup of coffee, saying, "Not much, mind you, but I just bought the coffee pot and figured how to make the coffee — my woman always did it — I just had to do somethin'."

He brushed a tear with the back of his workworn hand, and continued, "Cain't run no chicken farm without my woman — and all those young 'uns to tend."

Day after day I cared for "his woman," and spoke softly, "Don't be afraid, you will make it. God will take care of you. Your family is fine. People are praying for you."

Once again I quoted the 23rd Psalm — and there was a stir. My patient's eyes opened. "That voice . . . I . . . know that voice," she faltered. "I heard someone talking. *You are the voice!*"

"Yes," I answered with a lump in my throat. "I am the voice!"

She continued, "One day I felt like I was going through a long dark tunnel; then through cold, black water. I was so cold. Someone lifted me up and put a warm blanket under me." Her lip trembled, "Then I heard the voice, saying, 'Though I walk through the valley of the shadow of death, I will fear no evil for thou art with me.' I felt a warm hand pull me back. *I heard you!*"

Gradually the patient improved until she was able to sit in a chair. Until then only her husband was allowed to visit her but with Christmas coming, her children were to be allowed to visit two at a time on Christmas Day.

Her three nurses from the three shifts bought her a beautiful pink stole for the occasion. When Christmas morning came, my chicken farmer was there with the cup of coffee. By the time her children came, my patient was sitting in a chair, her long black hair parted and braided — with a pink bow in each braid. The soft stole around her shoulders covered a warm flannel robe. She was beautiful!

The farmer gave her an approving glance, then joked tenderly, "Now, now, we cain't be lettin' you git used to them fancy things."

She understood — and smiled up at him. And then her children were there. Her dark brown eyes filled with tears as the first two came through the door of her room. They came at intervals, quietly and in awe. Her married daughter and the young husband lingered the longest. Finally they left to take the younger children home.

"Your daughter is lovely," I said, when we were alone. "She seems to have a nice husband."

"He is a good boy," the mother answered; then

quietly added, "He just walks soft-like through life."

The day came when she went home to the farm.

Months later I had a surprise visit. There stood my chicken farmer in his clean overalls, his patient wife beside him. She was wearing a plain cotton dress and flat shoes. Her long black hair was pulled back into a bun. They stood hand in hand.

"Farm's goin' good, ma'am," he told me. "Young 'uns all in school. Right smart, too. It's good to have Ma home—just cain't run no chicken farm without my woman."

Her smile said it all—and somehow the memory goes "soft-like" through my life.

13

"DIAMONDS AND MINK, NO LESS!"

"I knew it! I knew it! I should have married Sammy!"

Suddenly our house was too small. The walls just seemed to close in on me. Five books had been hand-written on the kitchen table. Harold had typed those five books in the dining room. Boxes of notes and mail were jammed into a closet. It seemed the whole house had become an office.

My Norwegian heritage cried out for Scandinavian order!

Our organized daughter, Janice, shuddered at the boxes. "With all your speaking and traveling, you've got to have a place for files and desks."

Even Ralph recognized the need. "Mom, you just have to have an office!"

"I'll help you sort boxes, when you get your room,"

Ralph's wife Chris offered.

Harold added sheepishly, "I already bought a four-drawer file and a new desk at an auction. But everything is stacked on the porch."

Our new friends, Bob and Lou Marbry from New Jersey, were in on the family discussion.

Larry, their son, chimed in with, "We can do it! You get the material and I'll build. We can build a garage with an office in the back for Margaret. I'll draw up the plans."

Steve, our nephew, joined in, "Way to go! A room for the famous author."

"Well, Steve, if I'm so famous how come I only have one bathroom?" I stole a glance at Harold—I couldn't help it. I just had to say it: "I knew it! I knew it . . . I should have married Sammy!"

A long time ago when I was a young student nurse, I was assigned to a difficult patient who complained continuously.

"Oye, oye! Wash good between the toes, Blondie, not too often I get to the feet. Now my back—a good rub I should have. How I suffer with the back. Too much lifting I tell my Abie. But does he listen? All day I work in the deli, on my feet, no less, and who cares? I tell him all day my back hurts, but does he listen? So who listens?"

I would listen as I bathed her.

Then I would tell her stories. One story was about Mama and the red linoleum she bought for $1.00 because the corner was torn. "Believe me, a red linoleum is next to heaven after getting splinters in your hands from scrubbing wooden floors."

The "Oye, oye" stopped. My patient was listening. I rubbed her back — and continued.

"We had a water tank in the corner of the kitchen. The water wagon came twice a week and we got fresh water for 25 cents a barrel." I tied the top of her hospital gown, stretching it across her broad shoulders.

"Then there was the outhouse! It was so cold in the winter," I told her. "Blizzards and 60 below in Canada!"

She was lying on her back now, staring up at me.

"One day, when I was watching the children while Mama pulled the sled to the grocery store to get a bag of flour, the little ones had to use the potty.

"It was my duty to empty the potty in the outhouse, then rinse it with snow." I straightened the covers around my patient.

"Since it was so cold, I decided to empty the full potty into the cook stove." Her eyes widened. "The odor was terrible, but the worst part was that the fire went out. I had forgotten to put wood on the fire.

"Oye, oye," she exclaimed, squeezing her nostrils. "What'd your mama say?"

"I was only ten years old but I knew better. Well, of course when Mama came home, the fire was out and the kitchen didn't smell at all like Mama's kitchen. But before she had time to say a thing, the younger children announced in unison, 'Mama, Margaret emptied the potty in the stove.'"

My patient eased forward expectantly. "Did Mama spank, Blondie?" she asked sympathetically.

"Every family should have a lawyer and a doctor . . . " she looked long and hard at me, " . . . and a good nurse!"

I could barely force a smile, remembering. "No, Mama didn't have to spank. She just looked at me sadly and said, 'It is good when we can trust people, but it hurts when people don't fulfill that trust. You see, Margaret, disobedience hurts others. Emptying the potty in the stove may have seemed like a small thing, but it had big results. If you had put your coat on and gone out and emptied the potty in the outhouse, you might have remembered to get some wood for the stove.' "

The patient nodded in agreement, yet her sympathetic gaze never left my face.

"I learned a lesson that day when Mama said, 'Disobedience is never small in God's sight.' I understood, and I never emptied the potty in the stove again."

My patient's uproarious laugh split the air. "So now you empty bedpans!"

I didn't think she was funny at all!

Suddenly she sat up, and she was sympathetic again. "My Sammy, my wonderful Sammy! He is coming, and meet him you should. Och! So handsome! So smart! A lawyer he is—a smart lawyer. Every family should have a lawyer and a doctor . . . " she looked long and hard at me, " . . . and a good nurse!"

Clapping her hands together she closed her eyes, "Oye, I can see it now already—my grandchildren! What a beautiful couple you should make. Children you would have with the blonde hair and brown eyes— maybe blue eyes and black curly hair—a little like my hair, maybe? Diamonds and mink you should be wearing, Blondie. So handsome my Sammy—and rich! Abie and I spend nothing—all will go to Sammy."

"I will be happy to meet your Sammy." I tucked a pillow behind her back, confident that she would go to sleep dreaming about grandchildren.

I had a class, so I took a hurried leave and joined Hertha. I told her about Sammy, and we doubled up, laughing.

"She has grandchildren already and I haven't even met Sammy. I can't wait to tell Harold—diamonds and mink, no less!"

Then I met Sammy!

He was obese, stuffed in the chair, peering into a law book. His thick glasses sat low on his nose. He didn't budge out of the chair. I'm not sure he could have.

Over his glasses, he scrutinized me, top to toe. With a leering smile, he announced, "Mama, I like!"

She beamed. "See? What did I tell you, Blondie? So handsome, my Sammy. He likes!"

I choked on my silent laughter. "Oh, yes, I am pleased to meet your Sammy." He was still jammed in his chair. "But you see I must finish nurses' training."

"Finish? What's to finish? Marry my Sammy and

103

you don't nurse anymore. Maybe help in the deli — and give my back now and then . . . a little rub. Mink and diamonds my Sammy will buy." Sammy nodded.

"That is lovely, but I must go now. The hospital rules are very strict and I have a stubborn Norwegian father who insists that we finish what we begin."

Sammy sighed, and bent over his law books; the light shone on his bald spot . . .

That was more than fifty years ago. And ever since then, whenever the budget looks lean and we need a good laugh, I only have to say, "I should have married Sammy. Diamonds and mink, no less!"

Now the hammers are heard, concrete is being poured and walls are going up. By the time I begin my sixth book I will be in my own office with files in order and no boxes in the closet. And a special spot for Harold to type. I'll keep the coffee pot on — so come and see!

Diamonds and mink? Who needs them? Larry has promised me another bathroom — for the office.

14

THE KIDNEY STONE PLAYERS

*No one suspected the sense of humor
behind Ruth's starched efficiency.*

Memories come softly . . . gently . . . like a
pair of slippered feet, and I cry, and I laugh. The day
began so simply — just a letter. But the memories came,
unannounced, and stayed. I wrote:

Dear Ruth,
My heart weeps with you because of the empty
loneliness without Fred, yet, I know your faith in
God is strong. Still, we cry together . . .
Do you remember when we were young, and each
day was a new challenge? You and I saw life at its
best and its worst. We also laughed together.
I'll never forget when you and the O.R. nurse
wrote the play, "The Kidney Stone Players." Remember how Harold and Fred laughed? They didn't
think we could do it — but we did!
How did we ever have the nerve? I can see you
now . . .

Ruth Bremer, tall and stately with dark hair and eyes, was a Presbyterian minister's wife. She was also the director of nurses at the beautiful new Kennestone Hospital in Marietta, Georgia.

As her assistant, I stood in awe of her nursing and administrative skills. I also knew her as a friend! But no one suspected the sense of humor behind Ruth's starched efficiency.

The community of Marietta was changing and the new hospital brought modern methods into the old concepts of medical care. The townspeople looked down in suspicion on the unfamiliar equipment and updated procedures. As a result, they had been reluctant to accept what the hospital could do for them. To help unite the old and the new, Ruth and an O.R. nurse planned a comedy production. Even a few reluctant doctors were lured into the act.

They called themselves "The Kidney Stone Players," a play on the name of the new Kennestone Hospital. They opened the performances to the general public as well as the hospital staff, and this ridiculous skit became a turning point, bridging the gap and allowing the people's attitudes to relax. As the play was shown over and over, it transformed the community's response and the new hospital finally became a recognized part of the town.

Dignified Ruth Bremer was the main character, an irate patient in a doctor's office, complaining of an assortment of ailments. Her outlandish dress was matched by a large hat covered with ribbons and bells. She plunked a large, open jar down on the doctor's desk. "The nurse told me to bring a specimen of urine," she announced.

She flipped her hand exclaiming, "Such foolishness" — and accidentally knocked the jar over, spilling the "specimen" all over the doctor's desk.

The doctor admitted her to the hospital for observation.

A sloppily dressed aide, blowing bubble gum, escorted the patient to her room. In endless chatter the aide told of all her relatives who had died "right here in this hospital!"

The patient slept on while the doctors pulled out a string of sausage links. One doctor yelled, "Put that back! That's not it!"

In the next scene, an emergency developed in the lobby. A woman came in, obviously in advanced labor. In the excitement, the attendant shoved the father-to-be into the wheel chair and rushed him to the delivery room.

On another floor a doctor was ready to make rounds. "Where are all the nurses?" he shouted. From behind the door, I emerged in a uniform, fifty years too late, a crooked cap perched on my head — a coffee pot in one hand. With a heavy Norwegian accent, I answered, "I am on my coffee break."

"Well, a five-minute coffee break doesn't take all day," he snarled.

"Oh, ja, but I have coffee every hour on the hour, doctor."

With a look of disgust, he muttered, "I know there's a shortage of nurses, but this is ridiculous. Where did they find you?"

"Oh, ja, I come from Norvay. My tante Hilda taught me nursing."

Another scene showed the operating room. The nurses and doctors just rinsed their hands, pulled on old gloves, tied their shoelaces and then slipped into gowns and masks. During the surgery, a nurse bumped the instrument tray—dropping the instruments on the floor. She picked them up, wiped them on her gown, and replaced them on the tray.

The patient slept on, snoring loudly, while the doctors pulled out a string of sausage links. One doctor yelled, "Put that back! That's not it!"

In the last scene, I was back on stage with a pair of red-headed twin babies. "My tante Hilda knew it all the time!"

The finale: a chorus line of doctors in ruffled caps and drawers doing a song-and-dance routine. When they turned around and bowed, across the ruffles the audience read

THE   END

Then the curtain closed. Ruth came out on stage—hat and all—and glanced at Mel Wear, the hospital administrator, who was sitting on the front row. She asked sweetly, "Do we still have our jobs?"

I completed the letter to Ruth, licked the envelope

and sent it on its way. For the follower of God, grief eventually stretches the places of the heart, making room for compassion and laughter. I knew it would be that way with Ruth.

The Kidney Stone Players brought a comedy of errors, but the Emergency Room brought characters to life who should have been on the screen. Tragedy and comedy go together.

One day a man came into the Emergency Room and demanded recognition for inventing "thet thar penercillin." No one—but no one—gave him the time of day. Then the police came and gave him unexpected recognition.

When I catch a glimpse of a TV soap opera, I marvel at how any medical practice is accomplished at all.

In the Emergency Room we heard a story of two old farmers. One asked the other, "What's ailin' yur woman? I saw you tote her to the doc."

"Yep," the other farmer answered, "the doc done said she's got the flea-bitis—thet's what he says—'the flea-bitis' " (phlebitis).

"Law, man, thet ain't so bad. Jus' dip her like we do the hogs and sheep."

There were times in the E.R. when no one laughed, like the day a young child came in with his foot cut off. It had happened while he was riding a lawn mower. His father, overcome with remorse and grief, was treated for shock. (I still shudder when I see someone with bare feet mowing a lawn.)

The agony of life was always present in the E.R., but now and then comedy gave a needed balance. A farmer came in one day. "Doc, my woman has been ailin' — powerful smart — in her back. Reckon she done too much ironin'?"

Later I asked the doctor what was wrong with the patient.

"Oh, it wasn't the ironing," he chuckled. "She just delivered a baby boy."

One of the nurses told us about another farmer's pregnant wife who had gone out to slop the hogs. She climbed up the rail fence to dump her bucket into the hog trough, but lost her balance and lurched head first into the hog mire.

She went into labor, surrounded by squealing pigs slurping breakfast. She screamed for her husband who was in the barn. He lifted her up, laid her in the back of the pickup truck and raced for the hospital.

The baby was quickly delivered — the bath took a little longer.

At one time we had a "no-nonsense" nurse in the E.R. who resented any interruptions from family or visitors. Her brusque attitude was mistaken for rudeness. When she transferred to the Recovery Room, her "no-nonsense" approach was received thankfully by the doctors. Everyone has a place, and sometimes we miss the true worth of someone who is serving in the wrong situation.

One day a family of six came into the E.R. Diagnosis: hepatitis. Later, a friend of the nurses saw to it that food and clothing were given to the family.

On another day we heard of a family, living in the country, who all had pneumonia. A doctor found his way over the dirt road, and later, people from a nearby church sent a stove and wood, and food and clothing. Everyone in the family recovered.

When I catch a glimpse of the TV soap operas, I marvel at how any medical practice is accomplished at all. I only wish the scriptwriters could read the diaries of nurses and doctors who have seen real life.

The true romance of life is to see love in action in the valley of everyday living. Today we hear of young people struggling to find themselves. I grew up in a family and in a profession where the vast majority of doctors and nurses were losing themselves — in service. That is when we find purpose in living — when we are involved in giving.

15

NO BIG DEAL

---

*I turned around — my cap crooked and
dust all over my face and uniform — and
saw a quiet stranger.*

Beverly bounced through the kitchen door, laughing delightedly, "Aunt Margaret, wait until you hear this one!"

I put my pen down and in the dining room Harold stopped typing. It was time for a break anyway.

Beverly, a petite blonde, is married to Steve Jensen, our nephew. "Benjamin's first grade teacher just called and I thought, 'Oh, no! What's he done now?'"

Benjamin had not been feeling well one day and he had asked his teacher to call his mother. There was no answer. "I can't reach your mother right now," the teacher told Benjamin, "but we'll try again later."

Benjamin looked out the school window, then his

face brightened. "Oh, do you know Aunt Margaret, the author?" The teacher nodded as Benjamin continued. "She wrote *First We Have Coffee*—that book is about her mother. Then she wrote *Lena* and that is about Ralph. *First Comes the Wind* is a love story and *Papa's Place* is about Aunt Margaret's father. She's writing one now about nursing. Do you know my Aunt Margaret?" he repeated.

"I have read two of her books, but I certainly have learned something today."

"You have?"

"Oh, yes," the teacher told him. "I have learned about your Aunt Margaret, the author."

"Oh." Then he grew quiet. "Oh, well," he sighed, "when you get to know her, it's no big deal."

No big deal—he was right. Sometimes, when we think the agony of life is overwhelming, God allows the ecstasy. Somehow it all comes together, the rain and the sun, the smiles and the tears—all a part of life and not always the big deal we make it out to be.

It's a good thing, too. For instance, years ago we were expecting a new radiologist at the hospital so I had gathered a housecleaning crew together to reorganize supplies. Cleaning closets had been my thing since Miss Rosie days, so I scrambled up a ladder to clean out the old cast supplies on a top shelf.

A quiet voice behind me asked where the office was. Thinking he was one of the housekeeping crew, I suggested that he not stand there, but get busy and help clean up the department. "Can't you see we are trying to impress our new radiologist? Here's a box you can move into the office."

I turned around — my cap crooked and dust all over my face and uniform — and saw a dignified stranger. In a weak voice I added, "I don't think I know you. I am Margaret Jensen."

"I am Dr. Sanders, the new radiologist!"

Mountains and valleys — no big deal.

"Kathryn," I asked my granddaughter recently, "what do you want to be when you grow up?"

Katie's bright blue eyes twinkled and the bow seemed off balance in her tousled blond hair. She said, "A nurse, like my grammy. Then when I'm too old to do anything else, I'll write books — just like my grammy."

She blew me a kiss and skipped happily on her way. I wondered if she sensed at all how important nursing had been to me. It always was, even when I was six — like Kathryn.

I remembered one Sunday afternoon at the old parsonage on Ellen Street in Winnipeg, Manitoba. The house was quiet because everyone was taking a Sunday nap, including Papa.

My nap was always short, so Papa had given me instructions to be very quiet — and wait for a guest who was coming sometime that afternoon. "His name is Dr. Orchard," Papa said, "and he is the president of the Canadian Baptist Convention, so be sure you open the door, shake hands, and welcome him nicely. Can't forget your manners. Show Dr. Orchard a chair, and then come and get me. You don't need to say we are taking naps. Perhaps Canadians don't take naps on Sunday like Norwegians."

I promised!

Tired of waiting, I decided to play hospital. I got a couple of Mama's white sheets, put one on the parlor floor and covered the sofa with the other. Diapers made up the beds—all in a row—where imaginary babies were sleeping. I pinned a white diaper around my waist, and tied one around my head for my nurse's cap. With chart in hand, I went carefully from bed to bed, checking temperatures and duly recording the results.

Would she really follow in Grammy's footsteps? That would be a big deal to me.

During my routine hospital visit, a knock came at the front door. Suddenly, I was face to face with the president of the Canadian Baptist Convention.

I shook hands and told him my name, just as Papa said, and invited him to sit on my sheet-draped sofa. Proudly I told my guest, "Everyone except me is taking a nap"—then clapped my hand to my mouth—"Oh! Papa said I shouldn't say that. But that's what they are doing—taking naps. I don't like naps, but I had to take a little one!"

He was studying me seriously, his eyes sparkling.

"This is my hospital and I am the nurse. You see, when I grow up I'm going to be a nurse. And I'm going to write stories." My audience of one nodded his approval as I chatted on. "Papa thinks I tell too many

115

stories, but I tell stories to all my children."

Again, he nodded his approval.

"I have to pretend they are children. I don't have many toys. Papa threw my rag doll, Big Jack, in the furnace. Big Jack was so old, and Papa didn't know he was my only doll." I was standing directly in front of Dr. Orchard.

"Mama said I had to forgive Papa because he never had any toys and didn't know Big Jack was my friend. Poor Papa . . . no toys. I don't have toys, but I make up toys."

Dr. Orchard's voice was deep when he said, "It was good that you forgave your father." He smiled at my hospital. "So you are going to be a nurse, Margaret?"

I nodded my head confidently. "Oh, yes. See, these are all my sick children. Come . . . visit them," I urged. I tugged at his hand and together we made hospital visits.

Then Papa came downstairs! I had forgotten to call him! Papa's steely blue eyes looked straight through me — but Dr. Orchard saved the day!

"Pastor Tweten, you have a remarkable young daughter. She'll make a fine nurse, I'm sure."

I was still clutching Dr. Orchard's hand firmly. I needed a friend. I looked up at him and he winked.

"We have had a delightful visit and now we will close the hospital down, Margaret, so your father and I can visit."

Together we folded the diapers and sheets and we talked about sick children and nurses. Then I ran upstairs to tell Mama all about it.

Papa never mentioned the incident, but one day he returned from a Canadian Baptist Convention with, "Dr. Orchard sends his greetings to the little nurse, Margaret. Ja, ja, I wouldn't be surprised if you do become a nurse."

I watched my little Kathryn skipping happily in front of me — and I wondered, *would she really follow in Grammy's footsteps?* That *would* be a big deal to me.

Real importance, the really "big deals," grow out of love and commitment, the kind one elderly couple shared. A light rain drizzled on the metal awning outside the Emergency Room door of Kennestone Hospital. The earth was damp and the budding branches on the big oak reached out toward North Surgery. The hospital grounds were splotched with green, and friendly clouds hung close by.

It was almost time to go off duty and head for home. It seemed like a good day to transplant flower beds and dig in the moist earth. It certainly didn't look like a day for tragedy — but suddenly, there it was, sinister and black. A frightened old man shook with sobs as he was lifted gently from the ambulance. His little home, with all his worldly possessions, had just burned down. Tears streaked the soot on his cheeks. Ma stood quietly by — her gray hair, tied in a knot, framing her wrinkled face.

"Now, Pa, ain't no use in carryin' on so and gittin' yerself plumb tore up. I reckon it could be worse."

Pa sobbed, "But, Ma, you and me got nothin' in this world except what we got on our backs."

Ma's chin quivered; tears made a path in her furrowed cheeks. Her small gnarled arms wrapped around Pa and she buried her weary head against his whiskered chin. In a moment she suddenly straightened. "But, Pa," she said tenderly, "you got me and I got you, and we can work together. I still got strength in my legs and as long as I can stand up I can work." She turned to me. "Work's a blessing, Ma'am."

I nodded slowly, thinking how love suffers long and is kind, endures all things and always hopes. And another familiar passage came to mind: *I will never leave thee nor forsake thee.*

The doctor's kind words reassured the couple, and after a while they left the Emergency Room, hand in hand, walking into an unknown future.

The rain had stopped. The buds were dripping. The earth was soft. The clouds had lifted and the sun shone over the top. Love would find a way.

Commitment and covenant — *no big deal*. No, not when the heart settles it into the will from the very beginning.

16

GIFTS OF LOVE

"Margaret, you'll get what you want one way or the other. I might as well give you the warehouse."

The telephone lines were kept busy between North Carolina and Massachusetts. Heather, our eighteen-year-old granddaughter, had been taken to the Emergency Room at the hospital. X rays, tests, and surgery became the topic of conversation. All else was put aside — even writing. Across the country, family and friends prayed while waiting for the medical reports.

Dr. Bill Wood, noted surgeon, stopped his heavy schedule to sit and wait with the family. The gift of friendship comes in many wrappings.

Finally the sound of joy welled up when word came that Heather was going to be all right.

A family friend, Dr. Luke Sampson, stopped by

several weeks later for a cup of coffee and a visit. He recently had lost his mother and now he also was reliving the death of his young son, Jonathan.

His question burned into my heart. "But what if the reports had not been good—like in Jonathan's case? What would you have done then?"

I thought for a moment. "Luke, a thankful heart stores up past mercies to feed our faith in dark days. We can't *get* ready for tragedy. We must *stay* ready. The sting of death is cushioned by the fact that we are made for eternity. We can't avoid suffering and death, but we must bring it all into the light of eternity. We are made for eternity," I repeated. "This is just our training ground."

Thoughtfully my young friend responded, "We like to have control over our lives. And then something comes along that we have no control over. I'm beginning to realize that God in His sovereignty has a plan. Looking back, I can see in some measure how events can work together for good."

Faith is all that we can give to God—especially in the dark days. He gives us everything else—life, His covenant, the promises, above all His gift of love.

After Luke left, I thought back to another day, to experiences of the past which rekindle my faith today, to a number of gifts of love.

Ruth Bremer's nursing office was bursting with the news. Someone called out to me, "Rosa's house burned down! All her Christmas presents are gone. Her tree caught fire—everything's gone!"

My heart went out to Rosa, our faithful black maid,

who worked so diligently to keep her family together. I immediately reached for the telephone, and I called Frank Owenby, chairman of the hospital board, and owner of Owenbilt Mills. "We need help for Rosa. This is our opportunity to show that we are a family, and that we care. By the way, I have also been thinking about Christmas gifts for the children of the others on our housekeeping staff."

> *"Lord have mercy! Did you see how plumb carried away that child gets with a little wee? Ah do believe she's selling it!"*

There was a low chuckle on the other end of the line. Finally, Mr. Owenby answered, "You can have anything you want, Margaret. Just go to the warehouse and R. H. Witlock will show you the 'seconds' in clothes and you can fill the truck."

With a gentle laugh, he added, "Margaret, you'll get what you want one way or the other. I might as well give you the warehouse. You and Ruth Bremer—you're too much!" But his heart was as big as his warehouse.

We made a list of all the children: sizes and sex. We recruited help in finding a place and some furnishings for Rosa and her family. No hospital had a more exciting Christmas.

At the warehouse, I chose jackets and shirts— warm clothes—and even some baby things for the new twins. R. H. Whitlock filled the truck.

We used a room at the hospital to wrap and tag the

gifts. No one was forgotten. All was ready by the morning of Christmas Eve. It probably had never happened before and it might never happen again. But this was one moment in my life that keeps returning and rekindling my faith.

The smiles of joy, the heartfelt thanks and the sound of laughter brought a hospital family together. What had begun as a tragedy ended as a triumph.

I still remember one janitor who laid aside his mop and pail to show me a picture of his children in their new clothes.

When I saw Mr. Owenby later, I said, "How can I ever thank you?"

With a catch in his voice, he answered, "I should thank you. It was the happiest Christmas ever."

All through life we have the mountain peaks that give us a glimpse of the overall view. But for the most part, life is lived in the valleys of everyday tasks.

One of my tasks was to make rounds in the B section, the lower floor where black patients were admitted.

When I passed Miss Lizzie's room I called out a reminder to give us a urine specimen.

"Oh nurse, I forgot again — just went to the toilet." Lizzie, a diabetic, always forgot her morning specimen.

"I just need a few drops for testing — so how about trying one more time," I asked her.

She succeeded! I jokingly stood at attention, saluted, and cheered, "Hurrah for Miss Lizzie!"

The other women in the ward were laughing, and then I heard Miss Lizzie tell them, "Lord have mercy! Did you see how plumb carried away that child gets with a little wee? Ah do believe she's selling it!"

Across the hall was an elderly woman who had had surgery. I was trying to get her to sip a few swallows of ginger ale. "Come on now, Mammy, every little bit helps."

Sleepily, she answered, "That's what the old lady said when she wee'd in the ocean."

The men's ward was quiet — with the stillness of death. Three men in the four-bed ward were keeping watch. Uncle Joe, like fragile ebony, lay in a coma in the fourth bed, peaceful and quiet. His white hair framed his thin face. I checked his feeble pulse.

Uncle Joe, one hundred, more or less, was dying.

The silence was broken by one of the men. "Old Uncle Joe taught us how to read."

The others nodded.

"Never can get noplace if you can't read," he added.

They all agreed.

"Nurse," he said to me. "Uncle Joe, he taught us from the Bible — and all the young 'uns around — he read from the Bible, he did."

I saw that Uncle Joe's bed was soiled. I pulled the curtains and gave him a complete bath and changed his bedding.

When I finished, his frail, quiet form lay clean and

powdered in a spotless bed.

I pulled back the curtain, and saw that the three men were crying. "Thank you, nurse, the last wish Uncle Joe had was to be clean when he died. He wants to meet his Maker, clean."

The mountaintops in nursing were exhilarating, but the tasks in the valley brought peace.

Whenever we in the Emergency Room heard the wail of the ambulance, we braced ourselves for the unexpected. "Life is what happens to you while you are making other plans" should be inscribed over every Emergency Room door.

One day was quiet until we heard the wail, and we braced ourselves. A young husband had fallen asleep at the wheel of his car, and it hit a truck. His wife was admitted to surgery with severe lacerations. The two young children huddled beside their father in the waiting room, all in shock. They were enroute to Florida from a northern state.

I called Harold and he took the family to our home where they could wait more comfortably. They bathed and ate a good meal, and then fell asleep. Later, Harold retrieved the luggage from the wrecked car and called the insurance company for the worried young husband. When I got home we laundered all the blood-soaked clothes.

For a while I wondered what kind of people we had taken in — but not for long. Not when I overheard the four-year-old child tell the two-year-old, "Don't cry. Everything will be all right. I asked Jesus to help us, and *He did!*"

The young mother finally recovered and the entire family flew back home, but their gift of love—their friendship—remained.

Another morning, while I was arranging E.R. supplies for the day, I heard the screech of a car. A young girl dashed in, a limp baby in her arms. Sobbing hysterically, she cried, "She's dead! She's dead! Yesterday she was in a high chair and today my baby is dead."

A little later, the young woman's brother came to take her home. After they left, the doctor asked me to get an autopsy form filled out. "She was too upset now, Margaret, but I thought you could go and get it this afternoon, and also see how she is doing."

Ruth delivered what she thought was a stillborn. Then a faint gasp escaped from the tiny infant.

Another nurse and I drove out to the little house in the country where the mother lived. We got there just in time to hear an older woman, with arms folded, thunder forth, "Be sure your sins will find you out. You just had to go off with that no-good tramp and get yourself in the family way. Believe me, no sin will I tolerate in my house, and I told you to go!"

Anger rose up within me. I ordered the older woman to "be quiet"—and added, "I don't know what God you serve, but my God is a God of love and forgiveness. Your daughter lost someone precious to her, and I have come to see her."

The young mother fell into my arms and sobbed. After she grew quiet again, she signed the autopsy form. Cause of death: pneumonia. We talked about the future, and we became good friends. Later she went back to school, attended church and made new friends, took a secretarial course, and obtained a good job.

I'll always remember the kindness of this girl's young married brother who took her in when her own mother threw her out.

I will also remember a stormy night when Ruth Bremer was asked to travel a lonesome country road to a shack in the woods where a young girl was having her baby.

Ruth delivered what she thought was a stillborn. Then a faint gasp escaped from the tiny premature infant. Ruth immediately put the tiny baby inside her blouse and drove back to the hospital.

Somewhere today there is a black Ruth named after the Ruth who saved her life.

At the end of the hall in B section, I saw a doctor's mother sitting beside her black cook. The faithful old servant was dying and the *child* she had cared for was now her doctor, faithful in his care for her. The servant died peacefully, with her *family* around her, and the doctor's mother wept. Through her tears, she said to me, "You can't laugh together, weep together, pray together, and rear your children together and not love each other." She wiped her tears, saying, "I just lost my dear friend."

The time came when my days of nursing at Kennestone Hospital were drawing to a close. Harold and I were moving to North Carolina.

On one of my last rounds, I saw the housekeeping staff of the B section gathered together. They seemed to be led by one of the janitors, who used to be a butler in a wealthy home. He had brought his impeccable manners into his hospital job. He would greet me in the morning, bowing low. "Nurse, may I help you get your patient well by cleaning his room?"

"I would be honored," I would tell him.

When he finished I would thank him, and his reply was a thank you in return. Bowing with great dignity, he would say, "I appreciate your appreciation."

Somehow I had the feeling that wherever he went, he would always manage to poke holes in the darkness and let the sun shine through.

I wonder why we so often remember the small acts of kindness while the big events slip away.

That day, I looked at the huddled housekeeping staff and I asked, "What is wrong? Did someone die?"

They sadly shook their heads. Tears glistened on their black cheeks. "We just heard you were leaving." I suddenly realized they were crying for me! I cried, too!

The segregating walls could never segregate love, and I knew that one day even those walls would come down. With hugs and promises we parted. I shall never forget the gifts of love from B section.

17

COMES WINTER— COMES SPRING

"I have never in my life walked off a case, sir. This is going to make history."

The grey rain is falling gently on the tarpaper of the new roof. The ground is soggy and the garden from last year looks like a barren wilderness.

At least the roof is on and ready for the shingles, I thought to myself, *and I just have to believe that when summer comes the walks and driveway will be done, the gardens growing with flowers and the soggy, barren ground covered with lush green grass.*

"Faith is the . . . evidence of things not seen" (Hebrews 11:1). How often have I said that faith is a bridge that brings the invisible into the visible? Well, now I'm trying, really trying, to bring my hideaway room into the visible.

It is like nursing a critically ill patient and always

128

believing for a better day tomorrow. I never told a patient he would be *worse tomorrow*, but always said, "Tomorrow, you will be better." And I believed it.

But there was one day when I just knew *tomorrow would be worse.*

I carried a tray into the room where my patient sat. His tray held an attractive breakfast: fresh melon, poached egg and hot coffee — especially ordered for him. I really wanted to please him — he was my most difficult patient.

He cursed, "Take that tray away!" I exploded inside. (I remembered how my family had thanked God for oatmeal three times a day. We thought we were rich, and we prayed for the poor people.) I stood still, staring hard at my patient. "Well," he thundered, "what am I paying you for? This d--- hospital and these d--- doctors don't know what they are doing! Apparently you don't either!" He was angry — not just angry, but *angry* angry!

I picked up the tray and looked him right in the eye. "I have never in my life walked off a case, sir. This is going to make history. As of today, I am off this case. You don't need me, and I definitely don't need you! In fact, in all my years of nursing, you are the most obnoxious patient I have ever had." I grabbed a quick breath and added, "I will call the registry and get a replacement if there is one, but this is one nurse who is leaving!"

I stalked out — and bumped into his doctor. "Don't go in there yet," I warned. "I just started a revolution. I walked out!"

The doctor's expression registered shock. "You must be kidding! I've seen you nurse some mighty difficult cases and you never gave up before."

"Believe me, I did today. I just told him he was the most obnoxious patient I had ever nursed."

"You told the old man that?" He chuckled, "All these years I wanted to tell him that and now you, of all people — usually so patient — you really let him have it?"

"I did. You'd better not go in, doctor; just wait a few minutes. I'm calling the registry."

The doctor and I stood there, outside the door, looking at each other wide-eyed and speechless.

The doctor went down the hall to see his other patients while I made the call.

I couldn't believe it — no nurse available!

By that time the nurses at the desk knew that Jensen had told "Old Man X" off — and walked off the case. I became a heroine until they heard that the registry had no replacement.

"Oh, no," they moaned. "What if they can't get another nurse?"

I couldn't run off. I turned to the doctor. "Well, I guess I had better go back. If there's no nurse available, I'll have to stay the rest of the day. I certainly hope there will be a nurse by tomorrow."

The doctor and I walked back to Mr. X's room together. When we got there we stopped, dumbfounded. We heard: "Oh, Lord! Forgive me!" Mr. X was crying: "I am an obnoxious old man! Please let my nurse come back."

The doctor and I stood there, outside the door, looking at each other wide-eyed and speechless!

"I'll be thankful for my food, and I won't cuss anymore. Oh, Lord, let my nurse come back!"

With effort, we composed ourselves and walked into the room. "What's all the fuss about, Mr. X?" the doctor asked.

"I'm an obnoxious old man, that's what it is, and I'll mend my ways if only this *wonderful nurse* will stay. She just let me have it — and she is right."

So . . . I stayed. When the next tray arrived he prayed for five minutes, blessing everything on the tray — and his nurse. We became good friends, and we shared some difficult days since he was a very sick man. Every day he asked me to read the Bible to him.

One morning when I came on duty, his night nurse reported to me: "He became very ill last night and seemed to slip into a semi-coma. The resident doctor was called; then Mr. X improved. He slipped into a deep sleep, but he kept calling for you, Margaret. This morning he seems fine but he still keeps asking for you. No one is sure what happened."

When Mr. X and I were alone, he told me his side of the story. "I had a dream, a horrible nightmare. I was going down a tunnel and kept sliding toward hell. It was so real — hell was so very real, too horrible to describe.

I screamed for you, 'Please, Margaret! Help me up this slide!' But you weren't there. I kept screaming and sliding—down toward that horrible abyss, tortured by the sounds I was hearing."

I squeezed his hand to offer my comfort.

He barely noticed. "Just as I was about to fall in, I heard a voice say, 'I am the way, the truth, and the life.' When I turned I saw a beautiful cross. I reached toward the cross, Margaret, and a hand reached out to me and pulled me back up the slide. By then it was morning but I was still calling for you."

I squeezed his hand harder. "God, in His love, was speaking to you, Mr. X, even in a horrible nightmare."

"I know, I know," he answered softly. "But I have something to confess.

"When I was a young man, I was in a big revival meeting one evening. The preacher held an altar call and I went forward and gave my life to Jesus Christ. In the days that followed, I knew God had called me into the ministry." He trembled slightly. "But I realized the price I'd have to pay; I'd have to give up my lifestyle. I turned away from God's call, Margaret, and gave my life to obtaining wealth and social position."

I told him he didn't have to go on but he insisted.

"As the years passed, I turned away from my faith and became an obnoxious old man. I blamed everyone except me.

"But this morning I confessed to God and asked forgiveness. I came back to God, and for the first time in a long time I have peace in my heart. For my remaining time I will reach out with God's love to others around me."

The days that followed were days of peace and recovery. The Bible became Mr. X's constant companion. He lived several more years, and when he died he was at peace with God and man.

I read someplace that confession gives relief, but repentance brings release. That was true for Mr. X in that long ago time.

Tomorrow the sun will shine and the flowers will bloom and the grass will be green. When winter comes, the next thing to come is spring. And so it is with the winter of the soul; the next thing to come is hope — the spring of the heart.

18

PRIVATE DUTY NURSE

Life is filled with agony and ecstacy, but laughter is like a detergent.

"No one laughs anymore!" the young modern-day nurse declared.

She wearily complained to me how paper work and red tape, rules and regulations had the medical profession living on the ragged edge of frustration and burnout.

An elderly doctor spoke of the days before Intensive Care or Coronary Care units, when bedside nursing brought patients through crisis situations.

"We need both," he complained bitterly, "the new technology, *and* the personal touch. Too often the disease is treated but not the patient. When you 'old' private duty nurses are gone, Margaret, it will mark the end of an era of old-fashioned, bedside nursing. I am

glad I practiced medicine when I did," he told me.
"Somehow I don't fit into this age of computers and
transplants, to say nothing of sex changes. I'm over-
whelmed with the moral issues of abortion and sur-
rogate mothers. It seems to me we are complicating the
living and robbing the dying of dignity."

He moved sadly down the hall to visit an old friend,
a medical colleague of many days.

I knew what he meant. I've thought about it often.
He wore the unmistakable look of dignity that marked
the doctor of yesterday: dark suit, polished shoes, white
shirt and tie, his silver hair neatly parted. With a calm,
unhurried pace, he nodded his greeting to orderlies,
janitors, nurses and doctors. Gracious manners and
courtesy walked with him.

Change must come, I realize, but it is never easy.

I sighed and went to my patient's room. I had been
called to nurse an elderly patient who was blind, and
this would be my final case. After I met the patient and
family, I went to the desk to check the doctor's orders.
I asked for the head nurse. Before me stood a young
woman in a blue turtleneck sweater, slacks, unpolished
shoes — and no cap to identify her rank.

She looked at me as though I had arrived from
outer space. I was starched from cap to shoes.

"I am the head nurse!" she announced.

Then I saw her pin on her sweater.

Aides and orderlies were laughing down the hall.
A young man in blue jeans and a sweat shirt came to
the desk and wrote orders on the order sheet. He asked

for a prescription pad, and the nurse, still seated, just pointed to the drawer — she didn't even look up.

As I turned down the hall, I realized, *I've been around too long.* Then I met a friend from long ago. Her shoulders were stooped from years of nursing, but her cap was starched and her uniform crackled with stiffness. Her shoes were immaculate but her steps were slow as she moved softly down the hall.

"I'm nursing an old friend of mine," she confided. "I helped with all the babies in the family, and I nursed the old folks through the flu epidemic. Now old grandpa is dying and the family refused intensive care. They want a familiar face around him — so here I am; can't even retire." She chuckled delightedly.

"Did you see that head nurse?" I asked.

My friend nodded and whispered, "Remember how it used to be when the doctors came on the floor to make rounds? We all stood up and then the head nurse made rounds with him and took notes, and we had the dressing cart all ready."

"Believe me, I remember! Miss Rosie didn't miss a shoelace. What would she have done with a turtleneck sweater?"

We laughed together, and then went our separate ways. During the quiet of night duty, I looked out over the parking lot. A light rain was falling over the world outside. In the morning someone was to come and take my patient home. This would be my last night in the hospital where I had nursed for so many years. I would be packing my uniforms away.

The supervisors and head nurses I had known

were all retired. The older doctors had young assistants. One by one the older physicians were closing the door of their medical practice. In several cases a Doctor, Junior replaced the Doctor, Senior while the father beamed with pride. I wondered how many times I had heard a doctor say, "Nothing makes a father more proud than to have his son in the same profession." I agreed.

One by one, the private duty nurses were retiring; the young chose more dramatic areas of nursing. I was nostalgic by the time morning came. With the change of shifts (one old man called it the "swapping of the mules") I was fully prepared to go off duty for the last time. I passed the dining room on my way out and saw the long table where the private duty nurses used to eat together. Now aides and orderlies were drinking coffee there together.

I paused in the doorway, remembering. When we were on the day shift, a family member usually relieved us at 11:30 for lunch. That gave us time to get back before the patients' trays came.

For a moment I relived the story-telling that went on around that table. In thirty minutes we could eat lunch and hear a new story every day.

One elderly nurse told her own story. It happened during a serious flu epidemic when she was a young nurse. She went from case to case with little sleep. She barely had time to wash her uniforms and polish her shoes. The housework had to wait. Dishes piled up. The bed was left unmade and dust rolled without interruption.

One day she returned to her home and knew she, too, was very ill. She had the flu! She had seen several patients die. After weeks of nursing others, she was sure her resistance was too low to recover. There were no more doctors and nurses to call on. Everyone was exhausted.

She was going to die! She knew it.

Then she saw the disaster in her home.

"I will not have the women from First Church come in here and find me dead in this dirty house," she declared to the empty room. "This house will be put in a dying-clean condition!"

She prayed for strength to finish the job before she died — then proceeded to clean the bathroom, scrub the floors, wash the dishes, take out the garbage, and clean the refrigerator and stove.

Dragging herself to the bedroom, she changed the bed and put on her best sheets and embroidered pillow cases. She placed her soiled laundry in a laundry bag. Finally, everything was in order. After she bathed, she put on a warm flannel nightgown, brushed her hair, took some aspirin and sipped some hot tea.

"Now, I have this house in dying-clean condition," she declared. "Let the women of First Church come!"

By this time, her fever was soaring and she had chills. She crawled wearily into her clean bed. She folded her hands and prayed. She was ready to go.

Morning came! She was still in the same position, hands folded across her chest. The bed was drenched, her embroidered pillow cases damp from perspiration.

But her fever was gone. She opened her eyes. She was still alive!

I could hear again our laughter as we filled the elevator. We all vowed to go home and put our houses in "dying-clean condition."

The story we had just heard reminded me of some other moments of laughter. On one occasion, I was having difficulty in irrigating a colostomy.

A young doctor, who had not yet developed the virtue of patience, grabbed the equipment. "I'll show you how to irrigate."

"Wait a minute," I begged. "Let me get you a gown. This one is like a geyser."

"Don't tell me how to do a colostomy!" he growled.

Suddenly the geyser erupted and the handsome young doctor was showered with fecal material, from his glasses to his shoes.

Furiously, he headed for a shower, clothes and all, and ordered someone to call his wife to bring him a new wardrobe.

The colostomy patient's wonderful sense of humor helped her recovery. The doctor developed patience.

A young nurse, who had been sitting at another table, pushed into the elevator with us.

"You always have something to laugh about at your table," she said wistfully. "Everyone is so serious at our table. I don't see anything funny."

I replied, "That is sad! Life is filled with agony and ecstacy, but laughter is like a detergent. It clears the cobwebs from our minds. We see that for every thing there is a season: a time to weep, and a time to laugh.

"Make the most of your moments of laughter," I encouraged her, "for those moments will live in your memory."

Miss Ruthie thought for a moment, then her toothless smile lit up her face. "Hang her!"

The people in nursing homes often show a keen sense of humor. During one Sunday morning chapel service, as the wheelchairs rolled in, one little old lady yelled to another, "Your wheelchair touched mine!"

"No, it didn't!"

"Yes, it did!"

"Move over, then!"

An attendant moved the chair, and I chuckled to myself, thinking *They sound like my grandchildren.*

The preacher was a little late in arriving so this story-telling nurse was asked to fill in until he got there. In the middle of my story, one old lady called out, "Why don't you stop talking and let the preacher talk?"

Another interrupted her, "I think you are rude." Then several others got into the discussion.

The preacher came in, and the old lady announced, "About time!" Church continued.

Mama used to say, "We need one good laugh a

day." In a nursing home, you can't miss.

Miss Ruthie, for instance, was ninety years old, more or less, and moved about in her wheelchair with skill and ease. Her white hair was tied in a bow on top of her head; her grin revealed the humor in her heart.

A piano player often entertained the residents, and Miss Ruthie's feet kept time to the music.

"We ought to get married," she announced to the pianist one day.

"Well, Miss Ruthie, we all know how much I love you," answered the young piano player. "But there is a problem; I have a wife."

Miss Ruthie thought for a moment, then her toothless smile lit up her face. "Hang her!" she announced — and wheeled herself down the hall.

I left the hospital and moved toward my car in the parking lot. For the last time. An era in my life had come to an end. I heard a door close behind me.

Drops fell on the pavement, adding to the rain.

19

TODAY AND YESTERDAY

Pneumonia was the most fatal, and nursing care was the most important factor in caring for these patients.

"Grammy, you write your stories and I'll write in my diary." While I sat at my desk, six-year-old Kathryn took her pen in hand and sat beside me. She looked thoughtful—then began to write.

As I picked up my pen to write, too, I thought of Mr. B and the violets on his windowsill.

I glanced down at my grandchild, eager to tell her about him, but she was intent on the work at hand. She had her own stories to write—mine could wait. Someday I will tell her about the man who lay so near the edge of eternity, about the violets, and about how they were Jesus' special way of inviting a dying patient to "come to Me."

In a few moments, Kathryn tired of writing and dropped her pen. "Come on, Grammy," she urged. "Let's play dress-up."

Hand in hand we went to the old family chest. I took out some baby clothes. As I held up one tiny garment, I told her, "Your daddy wore this."

She eyed me skeptically.

Then she spotted something else. She frowned. "Grammy, what in the world is that?"

I leaned back. "That, my dear, is my nursing uniform from when I was a student nurse."

She stared at the uniform, then back at me. Picturing her daddy as small enough to wear a baby garment was tough enough. But picturing Grammy in that outfit was even harder.

She put on the blue and white striped uniform and time-worn apron, now yellowed with age. My cap was limp and grey — but I put it on her blond head.

"You wore this?" she giggled.

Then we took pictures! Soon it was bedtime. She curled up with her stuffed animals and I tucked her in. I wondered what she had written in her diary.

As she slept, pages from past years rustled in the dusty cupboards of my mind. On the bookshelf my textbooks stood in a row. *Anatomy and Physiology* (Kimber, Gray, Stackpole, 1934). I wondered what my grandchildren would be studying in the future. *Surgical Nursing* (Eliason, Ferguson, Lewis, 1934). I marvelled at the advanced technology of today.

I recall the time when I was six, and I helped the

143

doctor fix my blanket on the kitchen table. I climbed up on the blanket. Papa gave the chloroform and my tonsils were taken out — all on the kitchen table.

I opened the *Principles and Practice of Nursing* (1933) and saw a note from Mother Jensen (Harold's mother) that I had never noticed before. In her large scrawl she had written:

> *Life is a desert of thirst —*
> *But there are oases, and signs*
> *enough to find them.*

A second note read:

> *How confused the motives that guide our lives!*

I wondered when she had written those notes — and why I hadn't known her better. *Is it always so,* I asked myself, *that we fail to know each other?*

Another note said:

> *One can come into a room and it is as if another candle is lighted. Another comes — and we see the smoke and darkness.*

In still another, she had written:

> *Joy and exaltation, a white light on faces turned up to someone they adore. It is like the second movement of the ninth symphony. The music gets it clearer.*

The last note read:

> *Only one life, t'will soon be past;*
> *Only what's done for Christ will last.*
> — *Mother Jensen*

In her large handwriting she had penned these

words — so long ago — and I was just now discovering them!

She died in 1963, but before she went home she saw the heavens open and heard the music of angels. She was smiling when she closed her eyes. "Oh death, where is your sting?"

I turned the pages in my nursing book, and I stopped at the topic *Pneumonia.* I remembered the twenty-four-hour-duty nurses who stayed with their patients for twenty-four hours; then they would be relieved by a family member for four hours. Many of these patients had pneumonia.

Leona willed that child to life. Today Jeanelle is a beautiful grandmother.

Now I wonder how either the nurse or patient survived. Pneumonia was the most fatal of acute diseases and nursing care was the most important factor in caring for these patients — with mustard plaster paste, cupping, strapping the chest, and in some cases with venesection (blood letting; phlebotomy) and oxygen. The canvas tents they used were heavy and depressing.

The cold-air treatment was also used: The patient was wrapped well, including a hood — only his face exposed — then taken outside or into a cold room. A hot water bottle was placed at the feet. It almost reads like fiction today, but yesterday it was a frightening reality.

I remember when my one-month-old baby sister, Jeanelle, lay dying from pneumonia. Dr. Thornton's craggy face looked sad. "Give this one back to God, Mama," he advised. His shoulders sagged when he left. Grief is a heavy burden.

Leona, our nurse friend, took that blue baby and rubbed her with warm oil, suctioned out the mucous, and *willed* that child to life. Today, Jeanelle is a beautiful grandmother.

It was time to leave the books until another day. The principles remain unchanged, but the methods of practice change continually. Tragedy comes when principles change. Modern technology without eternal principles would bring malnutrition, starvation and death to the soul. In the medical world of yesterday or today, healing of spirit and soul as well as body is vital.

One case that defied medical explanation stands out vividly.

My cardiac patient was dying. The family was present and the intern had called the family physician who was already enroute from his home.

The patient's son had returned from military duty and sat weeping in the utility room. I reached out to comfort him, and he sobbed out his confession on my shoulder.

"Nurse, I kicked off family teaching . . . turned my back on my Christian training . . . just threw my life away. Now I realize what a fool I've been . . . and I want God's forgiveness . . . and my father's forgiveness."

We prayed together, amid the clatter of that utility room. Then he said, "Now it's too late; if only my dad knew. But now he's in a coma."

"Come on," I urged, "put your head in the oxygen tent and tell your father."

The son leaned into the tent, close to his father's cyanotic face. "Dad, Dad, I've come home — really home. I asked God to forgive me . . . and I want you to forgive me. I turned my life over to Jesus Christ . . . I love you, Dad!"

By the time the physician arrived, the patient's color was almost back to normal and he was calling out his son's name.

Months later I met the son again. "Guess what? I married a beautiful girl, and my dad is doing great!"

That memory from yesterday still brings joy today.

The morning after Kathryn had written in her diary, she sat down to enjoy a cup of milk and coffee with Papa, and she handed her diary to me. "Wanna see what I wrote, Grammy?"

I read, "I love you, Mom," on one page. The next page, "I love you, Dad." The following pages — "I love you . . . I love you . . . I love you . . . " She had named us all.

I opened God's diary. I turned the pages. His Word said the same thing to me: "I love you."

"Grammy, what are these old books?" Eric asked. He was helping me rearrange them on the shelves. I hadn't expected another "book day" so soon.

I dusted off *Obstetrics for Nurses* (written by Dr. DeLee in 1935). Inside the cover was a picture of a mother and her infant. The inscription read:

To the woman about to become a mother, or with

147

the newborn infant upon her bosom, wherever she bears her tender burden, this book is respectfully dedicated.

On page 219, I read about tuberculosis being the leading cause of death in the nation, the second being childbirth. About 23,000 women died every year in the United States from childbirth. Within the first four weeks of life, 100,000 babies died. That was three times the number of men lost in World War I. Yesterday.

Yesterday the mother's womb was the safest place for a baby; today that tiny baby has no defense.

Today we have Neonatal Intensive Care units and organ transplants — sophisticated medical equipment and skills — to save infants' lives, yet we allow unborn generations to be destroyed before birth, more than a million babies a year, more lives than in the holocaust.

Yesterday the mother's womb was the safest place for a baby; today that tiny baby has no defense.

When I was Eric's age, I didn't even know what the word *abortion* meant. Even in nurses' training I saw only two cases — and one of those girls died.

I'll never understand how we can spend unlimited funds to save a tiny premature baby outside the womb, yet deliberately destroy a baby inside the womb.

In my obstetrics book I read also that the time to get a new mother up was ten days after delivery. Some said three to four weeks. *A few said two to three days.* There are always a few who are ahead of their time.

Today, mothers are up within hours. Yesterday, fifty years ago, I saw a young mother die from an embolism on her tenth day.

Thumbing through another book, *Outline of Nursing History* (Goodnow, 1934), I saw pictures and statistics about nurses from around the world. They went back two hundred years: horse-drawn ambulances and army barracks, plagues and wars, death and disease. *Yesterday—in my nursing days—they were pictures and events. The only tears I shed were before or after an exam.*

Today I really saw the people, not just the pictures. We owe them so very much. My tears were real! Words like commitment, dedication, service, responsibility, courage, and faith rang out from those pages and I longed to hear those bells ringing clear today.

I want all of my grandchildren to know about Florence Nightingale. The book says that "the principles she laid down have never been improved upon." Methods may change. Principles must remain. It is said that we have ten million laws to enforce the Ten Commandments. The commandments can be torn from walls or textbooks, but God's laws remain unchanged, and can't be torn from our hearts.

Our little nine-year-old granddaughter Sarah is intrigued by the story of Florence Nightingale. Sarah's Grandfather Fisher was a descendant of that great lady, and Sarah carries the name: Sarah Elizabeth Nightingale Jensen—a long name for a little girl.

Sarah and I read about this elegant, tall, graceful woman from a wealthy home, who had a "call from

149

heaven" to care for the sick. Florence Nightingale believed that an earnest life must express itself in work for humanity and that "service of man is the service of God."

For years her parents kept her busy with travel and an active social life, hoping to discourage Florence from her dream. But when she was thirty-two, she finally persuaded her family to allow her to pursue her dream — to nurse, and to train others. In 1854 she set out for the Dardanelles with thirty-eight nurses. Using her own funds, and what she could solicit from friends, she arranged for nurses and medical supplies to be sent to the battle areas of the Crimean War. Even so, supplies were limited and conditions deplorable as those nurses cared for the wounded.

It said that no woman and few men in the world's history have planned such masterly undertakings in health programs and sanitation reforms. Florence's deep concern, her medical knowledge, and her political influence made her an excellent adviser to the United Kingdom on everything pertaining to hospitals and nursing.

She had been named Florence because she was born in Florence, Italy. But her wealthy and socially oriented parents were from England. She spoke Italian, German and French. Reaching her goals cost Florence her health, yet she lived to be ninety.

I didn't want to put the book down. Something within me cried out for heroines and heroes like her for today's youth. Today's stories are filled with youth and beauty, stardom and glamour, but where are the real heroes? Are they all hidden in dusty books? I looked at my granddaughter and said, "Sarah, I'm thankful you are reading about a true heroine."

I turned the pages and saw pictures of nurses around the world. One nurse in China cared for the victims of the great plague. She was dressed in a rubber-type jump suit, her shoes were covered, her face hidden by a hood and mask.

I remembered how my own father had seen six deaths in his family before he was nine years of age. All six had died from a disease called the "black sickness." After each death, a black cross was nailed on the door of their home. I'm sure Papa wondered if he would be next. Perhaps he feared someone would have to nail a black cross on the door in his memory.

I turned the pages and looked into the beautiful face of Edith Louisa Cavell, a British nurse in World War I who was executed by the Germans. Her crime? She saved lives—assisting more than two hundred Allied soldiers to escape to the Dutch border. A true heroine.

During the epidemic of typhus in Siberia about a half million people were affected, both rich and poor. People died in the roads. Within six months doctors and nurses from both America and Scotland brought medical relief. Sanitation was set up and tent wards were erected. Conditions improved. Unnamed heroes and heroines.

The book on nursing history included a story from the west where all but the father in a family of six died from diphtheria. The lonely farmer buried his entire family. Yesterday.

151

Today we are losing a great number of young men from AIDS — more, even, than in war.

Yesterday many of the plagues and contagious diseases came from germs no one could see. Then came penicillin and Salk vaccine and other miracle drugs.

Today we see an increase in the diseases which come from choice — not chance. Diet, liquor, tobacco and an undisciplined sexual lifestyle outside marriage cause so many of our nation's health problems. And the number keeps increasing. When we break away from God's laws, we lose control of our lives.

We had our heroes *yesterday* and we have them *today*. Our children need to be taught once again the basic principles that give us the heroes.

I put the book about nursing history on the shelf where it can be reached easily. I'm sure Heather will want to see those faces. I saw *pictures* fifty years ago. I have an idea she will see *people*.

EPILOG

MY TRIBUTE

I think it was Spurgeon who said, "Some of the storms of life come suddenly, a great sorrow or crushing defeat. Some come slowly. They appear on the ragged edges of the horizon, then overwhelm us. The history of manhood is always rough and rugged. No man is made without the storms.

"Great men, or women, preeminent because of their ability, were also made preeminent in suffering."

And in Tennyson we can read: "I am a part of all that I have met."

The places in my heart have been stretched by the men and women I have met; many of them within the walls of our great hospitals.

Norwegian American Hospital – Chicago, Illinois
Lutheran Deaconess Hospital – Chicago, Illinois
Kennestone Hospital – Marietta, Georgia
Moses Cone Memorial Hospital – Greensboro, North Carolina
Wesley Long Hospital – Greensboro, North Carolina
New Hanover Hospital – Wilmington, North Carolina
Cape Fear Hospital – Wilmington, North Carolina

From the dusty wings of my mind the doctors, nurses, and patients tiptoe across the stage of my heart.

The characters' faces are clear; the names are faded; the stories are true.

My caps and uniforms are laid aside. The white shoe polish is dry. A pen is in my hand, and across the stage of memory the players return—again and again.

My heart continues to applaud.

Old Doc Thornton, his craggy face with laughing eyes, his pink and blue pills, his shoulders bent beneath a bag of oranges for tired nurses—how can he be gone when I see him so clearly? He had put the wheels in motion when I confided in him that I wanted to be a nurse.

Miss Rosie, whose noble purpose still remains. Miss Hanna's disciplined training is being continued. Miss Abrahamson's quiet footsteps still echo down the hall.

I see the faces of my long-ago friends and classmates who have also packed away their uniforms; their white shoe polish has dried up, too. I think of the loving service, so unselfishly given; lonely hours of night duty; holidays surrendered. These will return in many ways to bless those who gave and those who received.

From out of the past the players continue to come across the stage: the housekeeping staff, the different hospital department personnel, the ambulance drivers, the policemen, the unsung heroes in life's drama. To the people who care for humanity's wounded, I thank you!

From my patients I learned much about courage

and faith. A special thanks to Dr. Robert Pigford for his humor and courage when he had to close his desk on an unfinished practice. Pain and forced leisure are trying companions.

Then I see, emerging from the shadows, the young, skilled medical men of today, with their new methods of practice. They, too, have hearts that cannot close. The principles remain unchanged.

"No day is lost when it holds a memory," I have read someplace. For me, every day holds at least one memory—so the years aren't really gone.

One day someone dropped this prayer into my bag saying, "I think you will like it." A man named Henry Edmond wrote it, and with it I close the book.

> May we come to the market place
> Out of the inner shrine.
> May we find the street
> Through the door of the temple.
> Give us to enter our place of service
> With the dew of worship on us.
> Let us bear about us the
> Fragrance of the Holy Place.
> May our approach be from above.

The following poem is dedicated to my friends and companions who have gone around the bend of the road ahead — toward home.

A Prayer

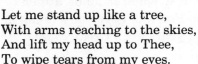

Don't let me shrivel up in tears
Or mildew in dark despair.
Don't let me dry up like the dust,
To blow away into the air.

Let me stand up like a tree,
With arms reaching to the skies,
And lift my head up to Thee,
To wipe tears from my eyes.

Don't let me cower low in fear,
Retreat into the quiet past;
Or live alone on memory,
Or dreams that cannot last.

Let me rise with strength anew
To hold love within my heart,
And turn again my steps to You,
And never from Your love depart.

Let me remember tender love,
Your gentle walk through life —
Your steadfast purpose from above
Contending faith — without the strife.

Remind me Lord, lest I forget
When days are long, nights are endless
To search for faces tears have wet,
Seek the lonely, or the friendless.

Remind me Lord, lest I forget
The road is closer now to home
We'll be together, where we met
Kneeling before the Father's throne.

— Margaret Tweten Jensen